UKULELE

CHORDS

MADE EASY

mobile
online
in print

Flame Tree
Music
BOOKS • eBOOKS • RESOURCES

Publisher and Creative Director: Nick Wells
Project, design and media integration: Jake Jackson
Website and software: David Neville with Stevens Dumpala and Steve Moulton
Editorial: Laura Bulbeck, Josie Mitchell, Gillian Whitaker

First published 2015 by
FLAME TREE PUBLISHING
6 Melbray Mews, Fulham
London, SW6 3NS
United Kingdom

www.flametreepublishing.com

Music information site: www.flametreemusic.com

15 17 19 18 16
1 3 5 7 9 10 8 6 4 2

Jake Jackson is a writer and musician. He has created and contributed to over 20 practical music books,
including *Reading Music Made Easy*, *Play Flamenco* and *Piano and Keyboard Chords*. His music is available
on iTunes, Amazon and Spotify amongst others.

ISBN: 978-1-78361-317-5

Printed in India

UKULELE CHORDS MADE EASY

SEE IT HEAR IT

ACCESSIBLE • HOW TO PLAY • RESOURCES

JAKE JACKSON

FLAME TREE
PUBLISHING

Contents

FREE ACCESS on smartphones
including iPhone & Android

Using any QR code app scan and **HEAR**
the chord on guitar and piano

A
A♯/B♭
B
C
C♯/D♭
D
D♯/E♭
E
F
F♯/G♭
G
G♯/A♭

Playing the Ukulele

Learning to play the ukulele can be fun and rewarding. Playing on your own, with friends, listening and playing along to songs, the ukulele is a great instrument to pick up and play.

The quickest way to start is to learn some chords. They are the building blocks of all musical compositions so we've tried to make the following pages as straightforward as possible, so you can start to play straightaway. The book is organised by key and offers you plenty of information to help you build your understanding. Each chord is clearly laid out, giving you the musical spelling, and the notes on each string of the instrument.

When you've learned the basics, you can start to practise chord shapes, and moving from one chord to the next. Online there are plenty of sources for music for popular and classic songs.

The C played on the open string above is **middle C** on a piano

About the Notes

Each step on the fretboard represents a note. Each note up the fretboard is higher than the one it precedes. The difference between each note is called an interval, and these intervals are used to make scales, which in turn are used to make chords.

Playing every note on a piano, from left to right, using all the white and the black keys, is similar to playing every note on every string from bass to treble strings on a guitar. A standard ukulele is slightly different because although every fret represents a different interval, the standard tuning of most ukuleles presents a G string that is only two intervals lower than the top, A string. This gives the ukulele its unique high-pitched tone and means that the root note of a chord (i.e. the note that gives the chord its name) is often on the 3rd string.

Right Hand Techniques

If you listen to a few songs you'll hear the time signatures, usually 4/4 for rock and pop, or 3/4 and 6/8 for other styles such as folk and country. For the ukulele there are two main techniques for the right hand: finger picking and strumming. The fingers offer a wider range of styles, but can be harder to learn at first (we've made one simple suggestion throughout this book, but many start with strumming which is a compelling percussive technique, suitable for playing with other instruments.

Here are a few strumming patterns to help you get started.

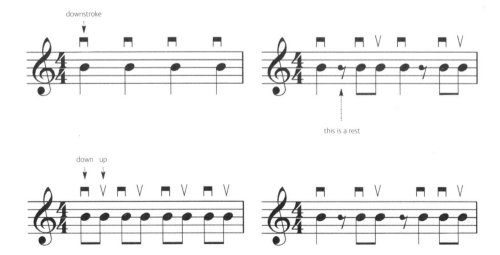

FREE ACCESS on smartphones including iPhone & Android   Using any QR code app scan and **HEAR** the chord on guitar and piano

7

Chord Diagrams
A Quick Guide

The chord diagram pages are designed for quick access and ease of use. You can flick through book using the tabs on the side to find the right key, then use the finger positions and fretboard to help you make the chord. Each chord is provided with a *Chord Spelling* on the page opposite the chord diagram, and will help you check each note. It's also is a great way to learn the structure of the sounds you're making and will help with melodies and playing with others. A simple arpeggio shape is also shown for right hand fingering.

The chord appears at the top of each page

Tabs help give quick access to the keys

Basic fingering with suggested motion, showing symbols for the fingers.

The Structure of each chord is shown here.

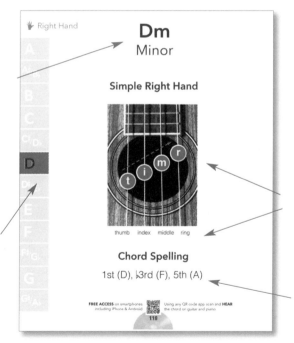

Chord Name:

Each chord is given a short and complete name, for example the short name C° is properly known as C Diminished

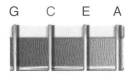

Left Hand Fingerings:

①   is the index finger

②   is the middle finger

③   is the ring finger

④   is the little finger

Tuning the Ukulele:

The open strings on a ukulele work in a different way to a guitar: the bottom string is just two notes lower than the top. This gives the characteristic jangling sound. Here are the same notes on a piano. Middle C in red.

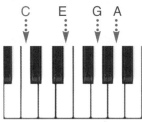

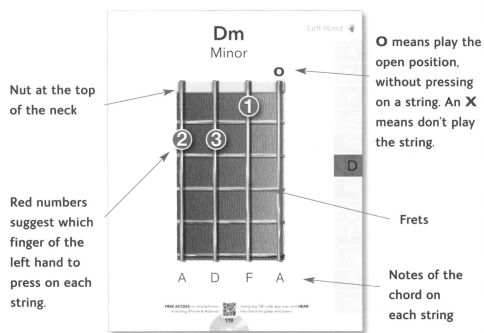

Nut at the top of the neck

O means play the open position, without pressing on a string. An **X** means don't play the string.

Frets

Red numbers suggest which finger of the left hand to press on each string.

Notes of the chord on each string

The Sound Links
A Quick Guide

Requirements: a camera and internet ready smartphone (eg. **iPhone**, any **Android** phone (e.g. **Samsung Galaxy**), **Nokia Lumia**, or **camera-enabled tablet** such as the **iPad Mini**). The best result is achieved using a WIFI connection.

1. Download any **free QR code reader**. An app store search will reveal a great many of these, so obviously its is best to go with the ones with the highest ratings and don't be afraid to try a few before you settle on the one that works best for you. Tapmedia's QR Reader app is good, or ATT Scanner (used below) or QR Media. Some of the free apps have ads, which can be annoying.

2. Find the chord you want to play, look at the diagram then check out the **QR code** at the base of the page.

FREE ACCESS on smartphones including iPhone & Android

Using any QR code app scan and **HEAR** the chord on guitar and piano

118

3. On your smartphone, open the app and **scan** the **QR code** at the base of any particular chord page.

4. The QR reader app will take you to a browser, then the specific chord will be displayed on the flametreemusic.com website.

FREE ACCESS on smartphones including iPhone & Android

Using any QR code app scan and **HEAR** the chord (e.g. this is C Major).

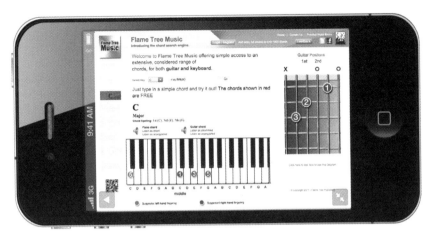

5. Using the usual pinch and zoom techniques, you can focus on four sound options.

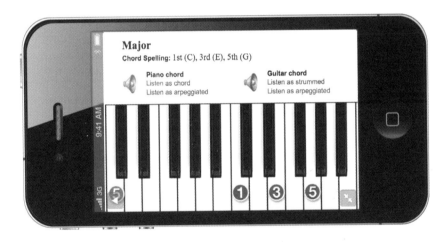

6. Click the sounds! Both piano and guitar audio is provided. This is particularly helpful when you're playing with others.

The QR codes give you direct access to all the chords. You can access a much wider range of chords if you register and subscribe.

FREE ACCESS on smartphones including iPhone & Android

Using any QR code app scan and **HEAR** the chord on guitar and piano

The Website
flametreemusic.com

The Flame Tree Music website is designed to make searching for chords very easy. It complements our range of print publications and offers easy access to chords online and on the move, through tablets, smartphones, desktop computers and books.

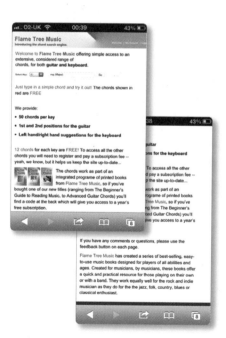

1. The site offers access to chord diagrams and finger positions for both the guitar and the piano/keyboard, presenting a wide range of sound options to help develop good listening technique, and to assist you in identifying the chord and each note within it.

2. The site offers 12 **free** chords, those most commonly used in a band setting or in songwriting.

3. A subscription is available for those who would like access to the full range of chords, **50** for **each key**.

FREE ACCESS on smartphones including iPhone & Android

Using any QR code app scan and **HEAR** the chord (e.g. this is C Major).

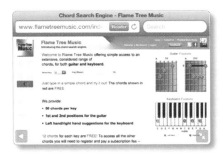

4. Guitar chords are shown with **first** and **second positions**.

5. For the keyboard, **left**- and **right-hand positions** are shown. The keyboard also sounds each note.

6. Choose the key, then the chord name from the drop down menu. Note that the **red chords** are available **free**. Those in blue can be accessed with a subscription.

7. Once you've selected the chord, press **GO** and the details of the chord will be shown, with chord spellings, keyboard and guitar fingerings.

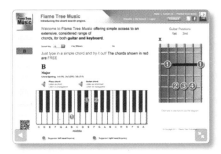

8. Initially, the first position for the guitar is shown. The second position can be selected by clicking the text above the chord diagram.

9. Sounds are provided in four easy-to-understand configurations.

The website is constantly evolving, so **further features will be added, including resources, scales and modes.**

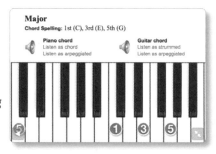

The Chords

FREE ACCESS on smartphones including iPhone & Android

Using any QR code app scan and **HEAR** the chord on guitar and piano

A
Major

A

A#/Bb

B

C

C#/Db

D

D#/Eb

E

F

F#/Gb

G

G#/Ab

Simple Right Hand

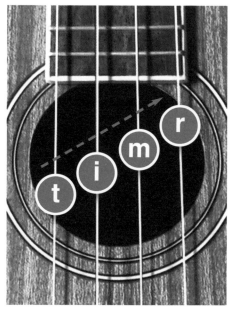

thumb   index   middle   ring

Chord Spelling

1st (A), 3rd (C#), 5th (E)

A
Major

A

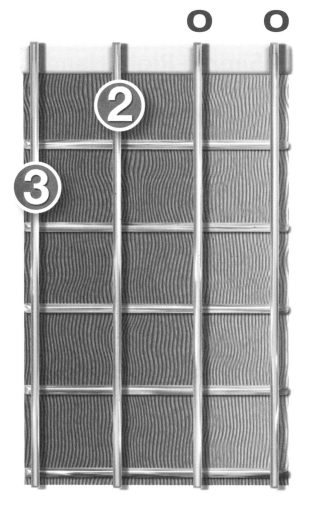

A   C#   E   A

FREE ACCESS on smartphones including iPhone & Android   Using any QR code app scan and **HEAR** the chord on guitar and piano

A
Minor

Simple Right Hand

thumb   index   middle   ring

Chord Spelling

1st (A), ♭3rd (C), 5th (E)

A
Minor

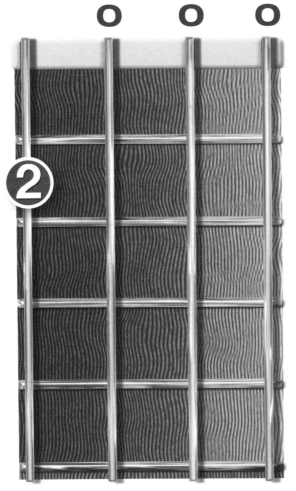

A   C   E   A

FREE ACCESS on smartphones including iPhone & Android

Using any QR code app scan and **HEAR** the chord on guitar and piano

A
A#/Bb
B
C
C#/Db
D
D#/Eb
E
F
F#/Gb
G
G#/Ab

A+
Augmented Triad

Simple Right Hand

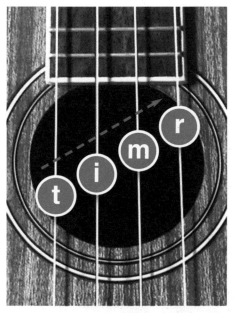

thumb   index   middle   ring

Chord Spelling

1st (A), 3rd (C#), #5th (E#)

A+
Augmented Triad

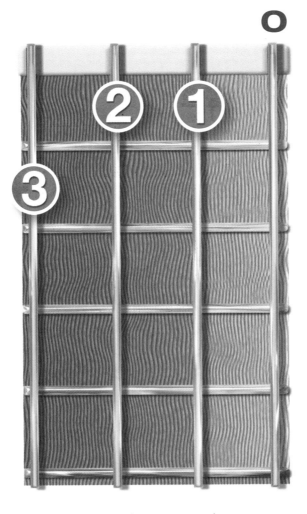

A   C#   E#   A

FREE ACCESS on smartphones including iPhone & Android

Using any QR code app scan and **HEAR** the chord on guitar and piano

A°
Diminished Triad

Simple Right Hand

thumb   index   middle   ring

Chord Spelling

1st (A), ♭3rd (C), ♭5th (E♭)

Using any QR code app scan and **HEAR**
the chord on guitar and piano

A°
Diminished Triad

x

A E♭ C

Asus2
Suspended 2nd

Simple Right Hand

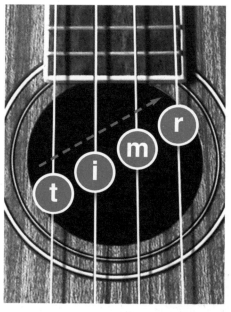

thumb   index   middle   ring

Chord Spelling

1st (A), 2nd (B), 5th (E)

Asus2
Suspended 2nd

O

② ③

④

A E E B

Asus4
Suspended 4th

Simple Right Hand

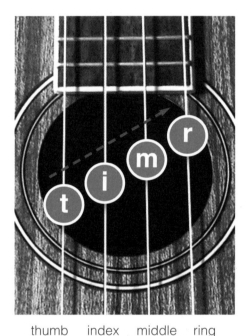

thumb   index   middle   ring

Chord Spelling
1st (A), 4th (D), 5th (E)

Asus4
Suspended 4th

A

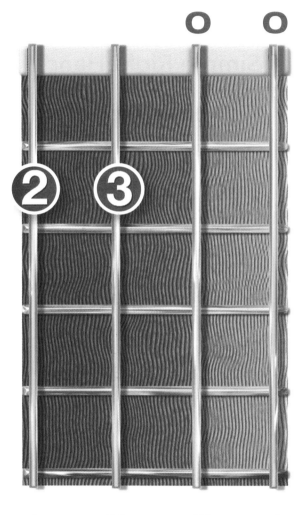

A   D   E   A

27

A

A6
Major 6th

Simple Right Hand

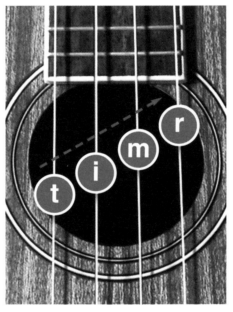

thumb   index   middle   ring

Chord Spelling

1st (A), 3rd (C♯), 5th (E), 6th (F♯)

A6
Major 6th

A   E   F♯   C♯

A

Amaj7
Major 7th

Simple Right Hand

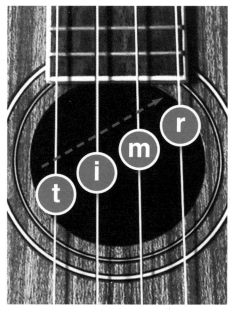

thumb   index   middle   ring

Chord Spelling

1st (A), 3rd (C♯), 5th (E), 7th (G♯)

Amaj7
Major 7th

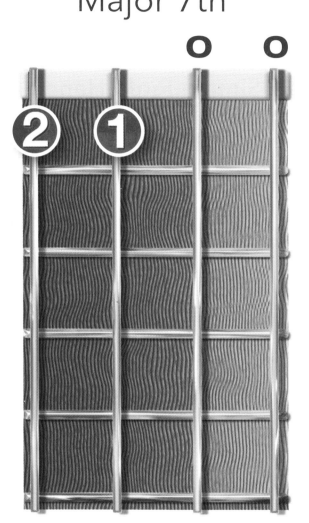

G♯   C♯   E   A

Am7
Minor 7th

Simple Right Hand

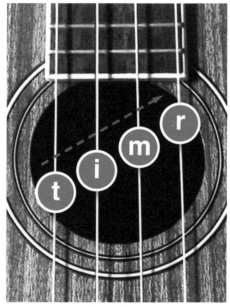

thumb   index   middle   ring

Chord Spelling

1st (A), ♭3rd (C), 5th (E), ♭7th (G)

Am7
Minor 7th

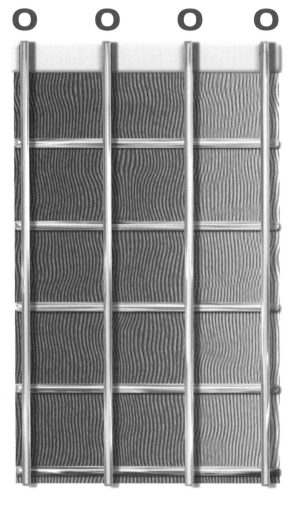

G   C   E   A

Right Hand

A

A7
Dominant 7th

Simple Right Hand

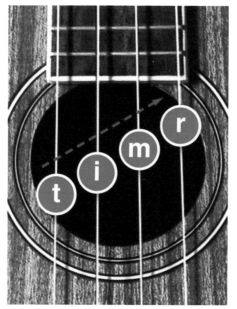

thumb   index   middle   ring

Chord Spelling

1st (A), 3rd (C♯), 5th (E), ♭7th (G)

FREE ACCESS on smartphones
including iPhone & Android

Using any QR code app scan and **HEAR**
the chord on guitar and piano

A7

Dominant 7th

G   C♯   E   A

A♯/B♭
Major

A♯/B♭

Simple Right Hand

thumb   index   middle   ring

Chord Spelling

1st (B♭), 3rd (D), 5th (F)

A#/B♭
Major

A#/B♭

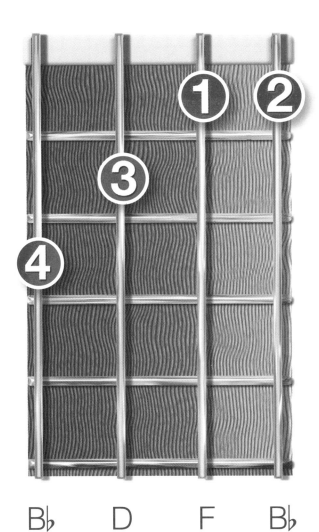

B♭   D   F   B♭

A♯/B♭m
Minor

Simple Right Hand

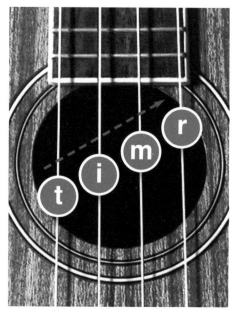

thumb   index   middle   ring

Chord Spelling

1st (B♭), ♭3rd (D♭), 5th (F)

A♯/B♭m
Minor

A♯/B♭

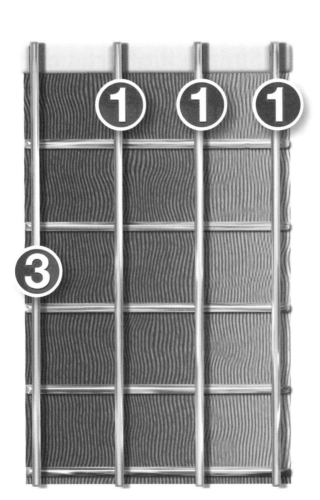

B♭   D♭   F   B♭

A♯/B♭+
Augmented Triad

A♯/B♭

Simple Right Hand

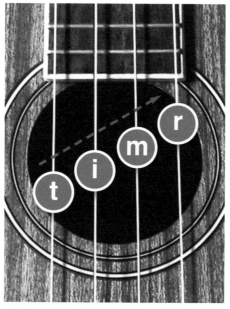

thumb   index   middle   ring

Chord Spelling

1st (B♭), 3rd (D), ♯5th (F♯)

A♯/B♭+
Augmented Triad

A
A♯/B♭
B
C
C♯/D♭
D
D♯/E♭
E
F
F♯/G♭
G
G♯/A♭

| B♭ | D | F♯ | B♭ |

A♯/B♭°
Diminished Triad

Simple Right Hand

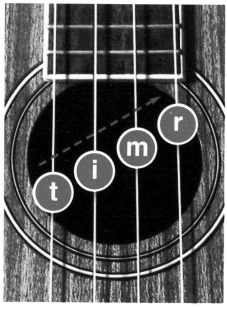

thumb   index   middle   ring

Chord Spelling

1st (B♭), ♭3rd (D♭), ♭5th (F♭)

A♯/B♭°
Diminished Triad

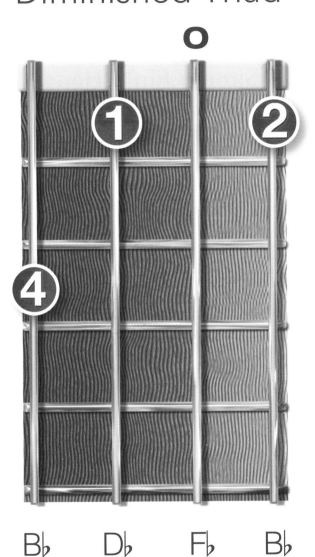

A♯/B♭

B♭   D♭   F♭   B♭

A♯/B♭sus2
Suspended 2nd

Simple Right Hand

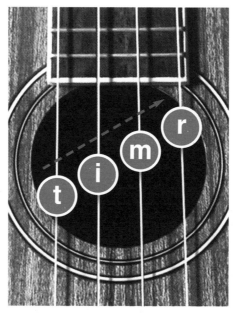

thumb   index   middle   ring

Chord Spelling

1st (B♭), 2nd (C), 5th (F)

A♯/B♭sus2
Suspended 2nd

A♯/B♭

O

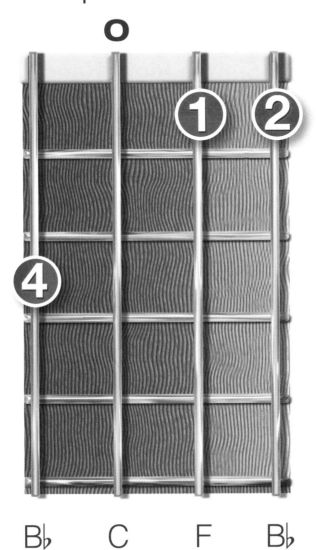

B♭   C   F   B♭

Using any QR code app scan and **HEAR** the chord on guitar and piano

A♯/B♭sus4
Suspended 4th

A♯/B♭

Simple Right Hand

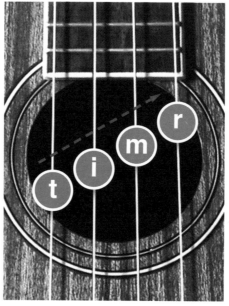

thumb   index   middle   ring

Chord Spelling

1st (B♭), 4th (E♭), 5th (F)

A♯/B♭sus4
Suspended 4th

A♯/B♭

B♭   E♭   F   B♭

Using any QR code app scan and **HEAR** the chord on guitar and piano

A♯/B♭6
Major 6th

A♯/B♭

Simple Right Hand

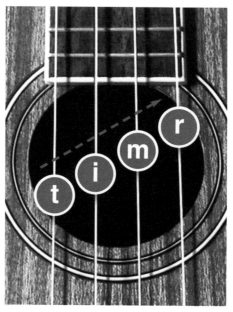

thumb   index   middle   ring

Chord Spelling

1st (B♭), 3rd (D), 5th (F), 6th (G)

A♯/B♭6
Major 6th

○

G   D   F   B♭

A♯/B♭maj7
Major 7th

A♯/B♭

Simple Right Hand

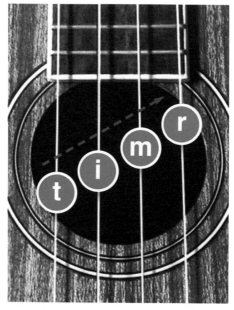

thumb   index   middle   ring

Chord Spelling
1st (B♭), 3rd (D), 5th (F), 7th (A)

A♯/B♭maj7
Major 7th

A   D   F   B♭

A♯/B♭m7
Minor 7th

A♯/B♭

Simple Right Hand

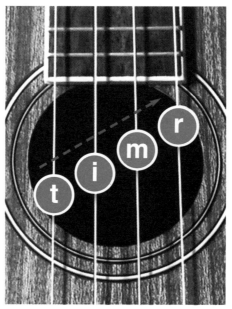

thumb   index   middle   ring

Chord Spelling
1st (B♭), ♭3rd (D♭), 5th (F), ♭7th (A♭)

A♯/B♭m7
Minor 7th

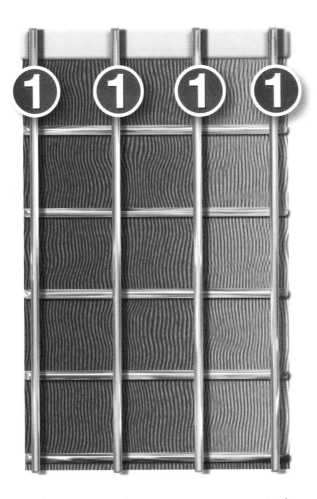

Ab   Db   F   Bb

A♯/B♭

A♯/B♭7
Dominant 7th

A♯/B♭

Simple Right Hand

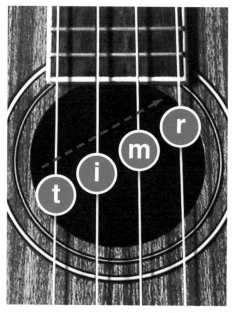

thumb   index   middle   ring

Chord Spelling

1st (B♭), 3rd (D), 5th (F), ♭7th (A♭)

A♯/B♭7
Dominant 7th

A♯/B♭

A♭   D   F   B♭

B
Major

Simple Right Hand

thumb   index   middle   ring

Chord Spelling

1st (B), 3rd (D♯), 5th (F♯)

A
A♯/B♭
B
C
C♯/D♭
D
D♯/E♭
E
F
F♯/G♭
G
G♯/A♭

B
Major

B   D♯   F♯   B

FREE ACCESS on smartphones
including iPhone & Android

Using any QR code app scan and **HEAR**
the chord on guitar and piano

Bm
Minor

Simple Right Hand

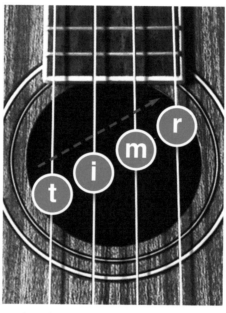

thumb   index   middle   ring

Chord Spelling
1st (B), ♭3rd (D), 5th (F♯)

Bm

Minor

B

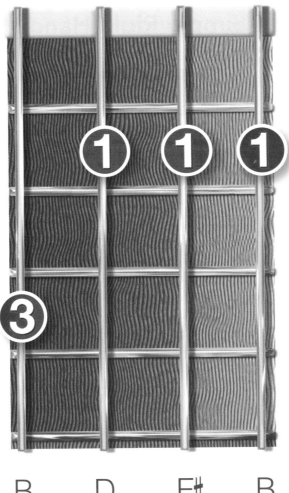

B   D   F♯   B

FREE ACCESS on smartphones including iPhone & Android

Using any QR code app scan and **HEAR** the chord on guitar and piano

59

 Right Hand

B+
Augmented Triad

Simple Right Hand

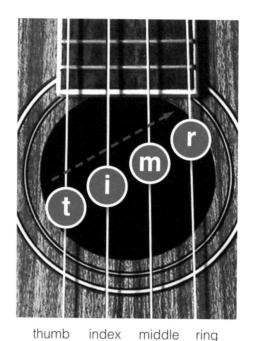

thumb   index   middle   ring

Chord Spelling
1st (B), 3rd (D♯), ♯5th (Fx)

B+
Augmented Triad

B   D#   Fx   B

B°
Diminished Triad

B

Simple Right Hand

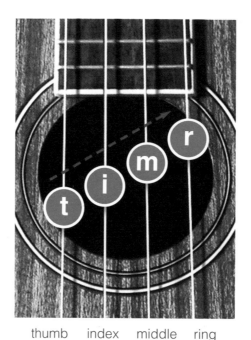

thumb   index   middle   ring

Chord Spelling

1st (B), ♭3rd (D), ♭5th (F)

B°
Diminished Triad

B

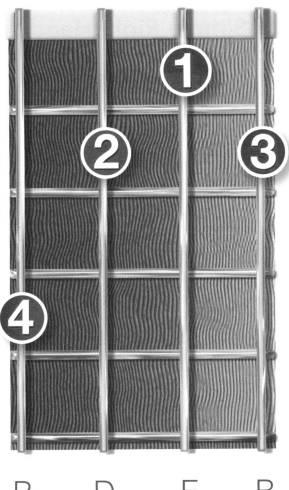

B   D   F   B

FREE ACCESS on smartphones including iPhone & Android

Using any QR code app scan and **HEAR** the chord on guitar and piano

Bsus2
Suspended 2nd

A
A♭/B♭
B
C
C♯/D♭
D
D♯/E♭
E
F
F♯/G♭
G
G♯/A♭

Simple Right Hand

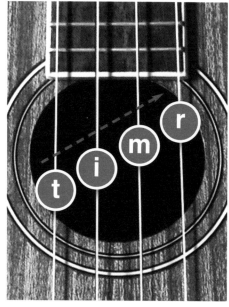

thumb index middle ring

Chord Spelling

1st (B), 2nd (C♯), 5th (F♯)

Bsus2
Suspended 2nd

B

B   C#   F#   B

Using any QR code app scan and **HEAR** the chord on guitar and piano

Bsus4
Suspended 4th

A
A♯/B♭
B
C
C♯/D♭
D
D♯/E♭
E
F
F♯/G♭
G
G♯/A♭

Simple Right Hand

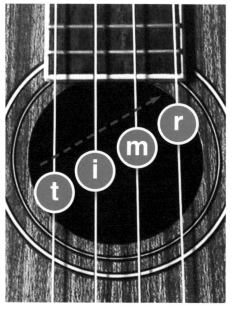

thumb   index   middle   ring

Chord Spelling

1st (B), 4th (E), 5th (F♯)

Bsus4
Suspended 4th

B

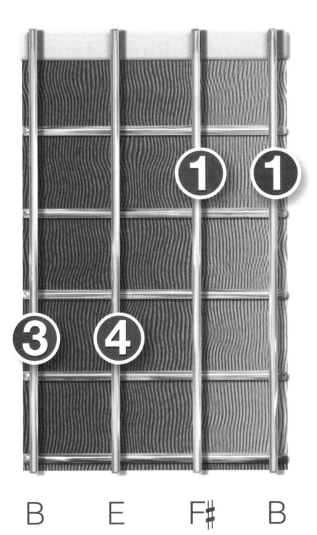

B　E　F♯　B

B6
Major 6th

A
A#/Bb
B
C
C#/Db
D
D#/Eb
E
F
F#/Gb
G
G#/Ab

Simple Right Hand

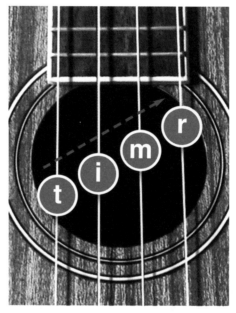

thumb   index   middle   ring

Chord Spelling

1st (B), 3rd (D♯), 5th (F♯), 6th (G♯)

B6
Major 6th

B

G#   D#   F#   B

Bmaj7
Major 7th

Simple Right Hand

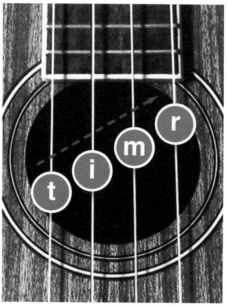

thumb   index   middle   ring

Chord Spelling

1st (B), 3rd (D♯), 5th (F♯), 7th (A♯)

B

Bmaj7
Major 7th

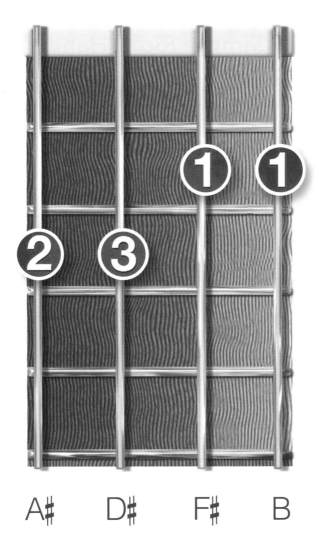

B

A#   D#   F#   B

Bm7
Minor 7th

Simple Right Hand

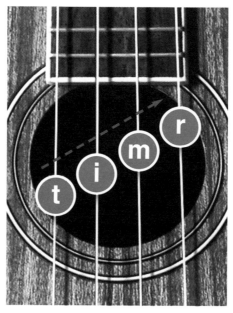

thumb   index   middle   ring

Chord Spelling

1st (B), ♭3rd (D), 5th (F♯), ♭7th (A)

B

A/A♭
A/B♭
B
C
C♯/D♭
D
D♯/E♭
E
F
F♯/G♭
G
G♯/A♭

Bm7
Minor 7th

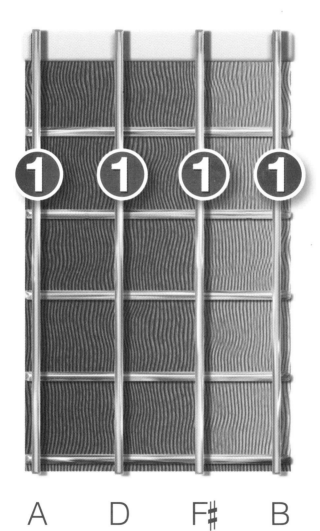

A   D   F♯   B

A

A♯/B♭

B

C

C♯/D♭

D

D♯/E♭

E

F

F♯/G♭

G

G♯/A♭

FREE ACCESS on smartphones including iPhone & Android

Using any QR code app scan and **HEAR** the chord on guitar and piano

B7
Dominant 7th

Simple Right Hand

thumb   index   middle   ring

Chord Spelling

1st (B), 3rd (D♯), 5th (F♯), ♭7th (A)

B7
Dominant 7th

B

A   D♯   F♯   B

FREE ACCESS on smartphones
including iPhone & Android

Using any QR code app scan and **HEAR**
the chord on guitar and piano

75

C
Major

Simple Right Hand

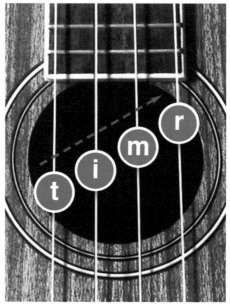

thumb   index   middle   ring

Chord Spelling
1st (C), 3rd (E), 5th (G)

C
Major

C

O   O   O

③

G   C   E   C

FREE ACCESS on smartphones including iPhone & Android

Using any QR code app scan and **HEAR** the chord on guitar and piano

Cm
Minor

Simple Right Hand

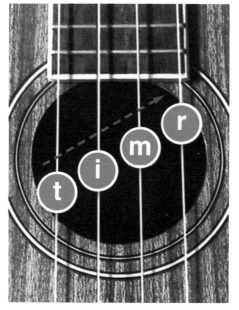

thumb   index   middle   ring

Chord Spelling

1st (C), ♭3rd (E♭), 5th (G)

Cm
Minor

G   E♭   G   C

FREE ACCESS on smartphones including iPhone & Android

Using any QR code app scan and **HEAR** the chord on guitar and piano

C+
Augmented Triad

Simple Right Hand

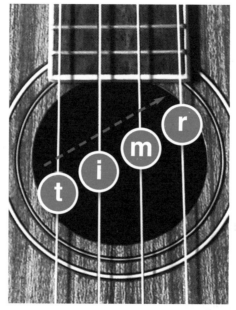

thumb   index   middle   ring

Chord Spelling

1st (C), 3rd (E), #5th (G#)

C+
Augmented Triad

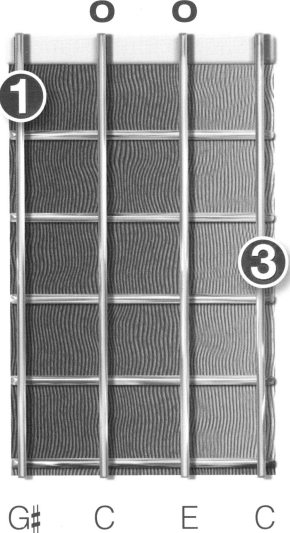

C

G♯   C   E   C

C°
Diminished Triad

Simple Right Hand

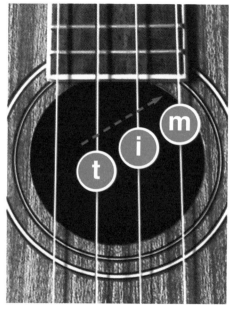

thumb   index   middle

Chord Spelling

1st (C), ♭3rd (E♭), ♭5th (G♭)

A
A♯/B♭
B
C
C♯/D♭
D
D♯/E♭
E
F
F♯/G♭
G
G♯/A♭

C°

Diminished Triad

C

Eb   Gb   C

Csus2
Suspended 2nd

Simple Right Hand

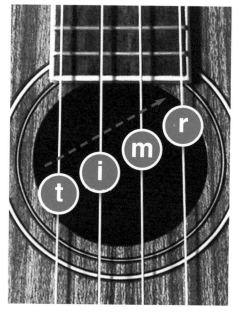

thumb   index   middle   ring

Chord Spelling

1st (C), 2nd (D), 5th (G)

Csus2
Suspended 2nd

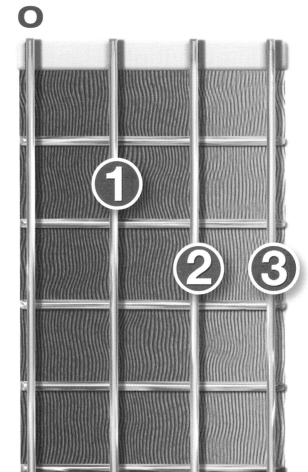

C

G   D   G   C

Csus4
Suspended 4th

C

Simple Right Hand

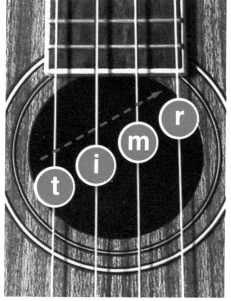

thumb   index   middle   ring

Chord Spelling
1st (C), 4th (F), 5th (G)

Csus4
Suspended 4th

C

G   C   F   C

FREE ACCESS on smartphones including iPhone & Android

Using any QR code app scan and **HEAR** the chord on guitar and piano

C6
Major 6th

Simple Right Hand

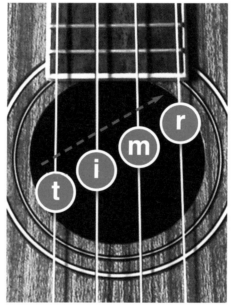

thumb   index   middle   ring

Chord Spelling
1st (C), 3rd (E), 5th (G), 6th (A)

C6
Major 6th

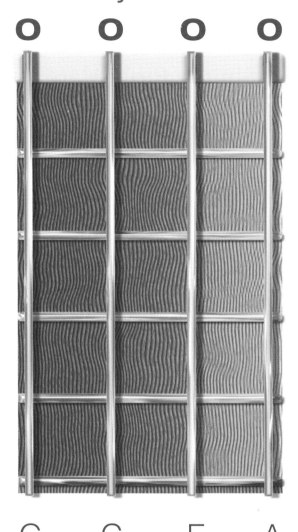

G   C   E   A

Cmaj7
Major 7th

Simple Right Hand

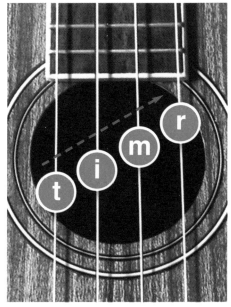

thumb   index   middle   ring

Chord Spelling

1st (C), 3rd (E), 5th (G), 7th (B)

Cmaj7
Major 7th

Left Hand ✋

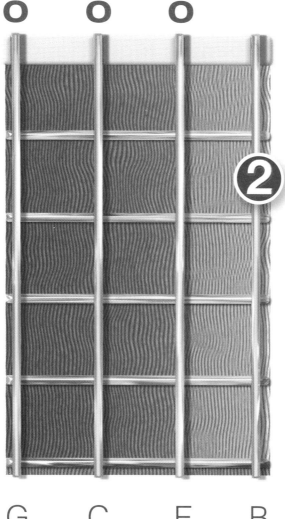

C

G C E B

Cm7
Minor 7th

Simple Right Hand

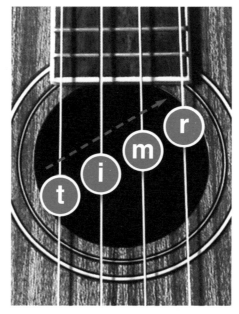

thumb   index   middle   ring

Chord Spelling

1st (C), ♭3rd (E♭), 5th (G), ♭7th (B♭)

Cm7
Minor 7th

C

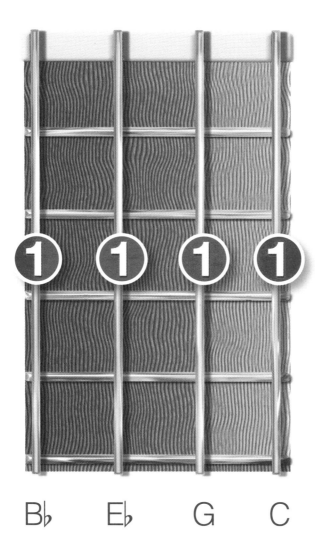

B♭   E♭   G   C

C7
Dominant 7th

Simple Right Hand

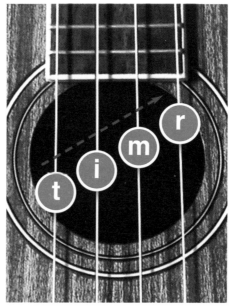

thumb   index   middle   ring

Chord Spelling

1st (C), 3rd (E), 5th (G), ♭7th (B♭)

C7
Dominant 7th

C

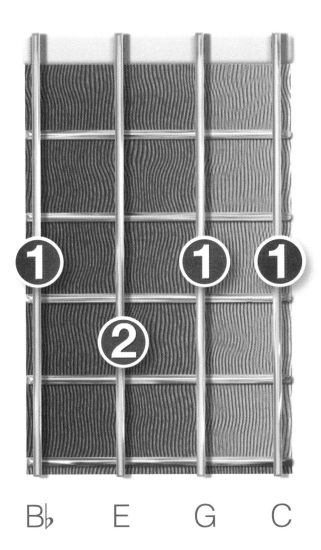

Bb E G C

C♯/D♭
Major

C♯/D♭

Simple Right Hand

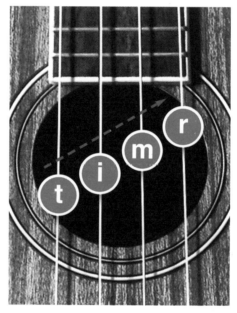

thumb   index   middle   ring

Chord Spelling
1st (C♯), 3rd (E♯), 5th (G♯)

C#/D♭
Major

G#   C#   E#   C#

C♯/D♭m
Minor

A
A♯/B♭
B
C
C♯/D♭
D
D♯/E♭
E
F
F♯/G♭
G
A♭/G♯

Simple Right Hand

thumb   index   middle   ring

Chord Spelling
1st (C♯), ♭3rd (E), 5th (G♯)

C#/D♭m
Minor

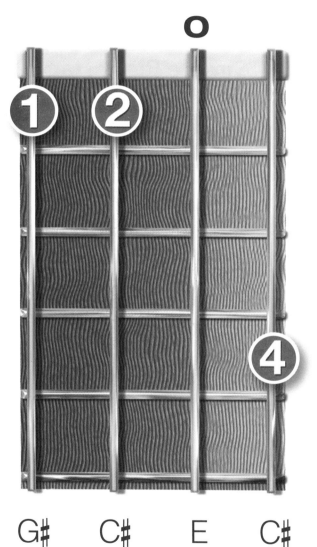

O

① ② ④

G# C# E C#

FREE ACCESS on smartphones including iPhone & Android

Using any QR code app scan and **HEAR** the chord on guitar and piano

C♯/D♭+
Augmented Triad

Simple Right Hand

thumb   index   middle   ring

Chord Spelling

1st (C♯), 3rd (E♯), ♯5th (Gx)

C♯/D♭+
Augmented Triad

Gx　　C♯　　E♯　　C♯

C♯/D♭

 Right Hand

C♯/D♭°
Diminished Triad

Simple Right Hand

thumb   index   middle   ring

Chord Spelling

1st (C♯), ♭3rd (E), ♭5th (G)

A

A♯/B♭

B

C

C♯/D♭

D

D♯/E♭

E

F

F♯/G♭

G

A♭/G♯

C#/D♭°
Diminished Triad

O   O

G   C#   E   C#

C#/D♭

 Right Hand

C♯/D♭sus2
Suspended 2nd

Simple Right Hand

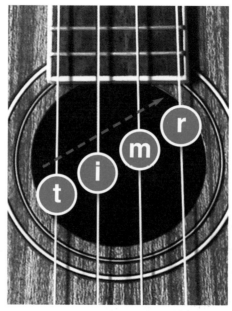

thumb   index   middle   ring

Chord Spelling

1st (C♯), 2nd (D♯), 5th (G♯)

FREE ACCESS on smartphones including iPhone & Android

Using any QR code app scan and **HEAR** the chord on guitar and piano

C#/D♭sus2
Suspended 2nd

C#/D♭

G#   D#   G#   C#

C#/D♭sus4
Suspended 4th

A
A#/B♭
B
C
C#/D♭
D
D#/E♭
E
F
F#/G♭
G
A♭/G#

Simple Right Hand

thumb   index   middle   ring

Chord Spelling

1st (C#), 4th (F#), 5th (G#)

C#/D♭sus4
Suspended 4th

C#/D♭

G#   C#   F#   C#

Right Hand

C#/D♭6
Major 6th

Simple Right Hand

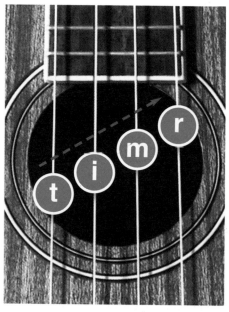

thumb   index   middle   ring

Chord Spelling

1st (C#), 3rd (E#), 5th (G#), 6th (A#)

FREE ACCESS on smartphones including iPhone & Android

Using any QR code app scan and **HEAR** the chord on guitar and piano

C#/Db6
Major 6th

C#/Db

G#   C#   E#   A#

C#/D♭maj7
Major 7th

Simple Right Hand

thumb   index   middle   ring

Chord Spelling

1st (C#), 3rd (E#), 5th (G#), 7th (B#)

A
A#/B♭
B
C
C#/D♭
D
D#/E♭
E
F
F#/G♭
G
A♭/G#

C#/D♭maj7
Major 7th

G#   C#   E#   B#

C#/D♭

FREE ACCESS on smartphones
including iPhone & Android

Using any QR code app scan and **HEAR**
the chord on guitar and piano

C#/D♭m7
Minor 7th

A
A#/B♭
B
C
C#/D♭
D
D#/E♭
E
F
F#/G♭
G
A♭/G#

Simple Right Hand

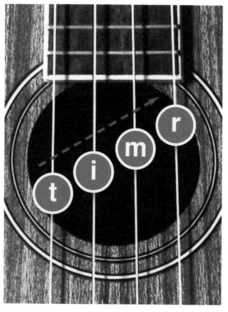

thumb   index   middle   ring

Chord Spelling

1st (C#), ♭3rd (E), 5th (G#), ♭7th (B)

FREE ACCESS on smartphones including iPhone & Android

Using any QR code app scan and **HEAR** the chord on guitar and piano

C♯/D♭m7
Minor 7th

Left Hand

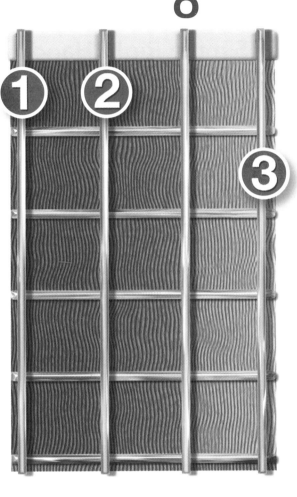

G♯   C♯   E   B

C♯/D♭

FREE ACCESS on smartphones including iPhone & Android

Using any QR code app scan and **HEAR** the chord on guitar and piano

113

C#/D♭7
Dominant 7th

A

A#/B♭

B

C

C#/D♭

D

D#/E♭

E

F

F#/G♭

G

A♭/G#

Simple Right Hand

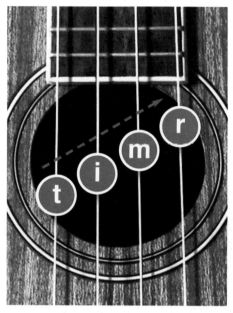

thumb   index   middle   ring

Chord Spelling

1st (C#), 3rd (E#), 5th (G#), ♭7th (B)

C#/Db7
Dominant 7th

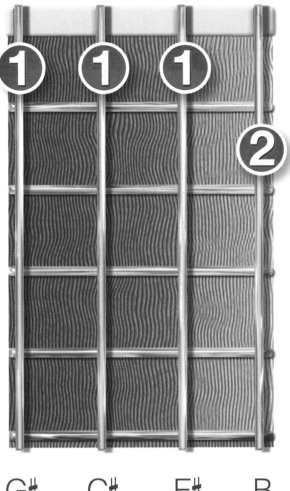

C#/Db

G#   C#   E#   B

FREE ACCESS on smartphones including iPhone & Android

Using any QR code app scan and **HEAR** the chord on guitar and piano

D
Major

A
A#/Bb
B
C
C#/Db
D
D#/Eb
E
F
F#/Gb
G
G#/Ab

Simple Right Hand

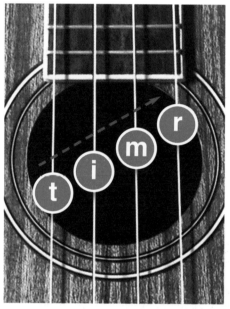

thumb   index   middle   ring

Chord Spelling
1st (D), 3rd (F♯), 5th (A)

D
Major

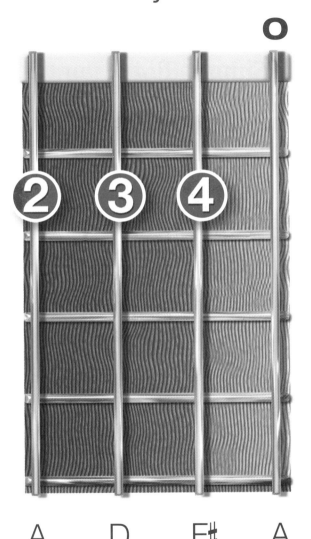

A   D   F♯   A

Dm
Minor

A
A♯/B♭
B
C
C♯/D♭
D
D♯/E♭
E
F
F♯/G♭
G
G♯/A♭

Simple Right Hand

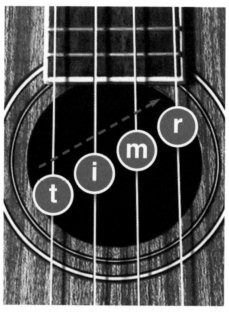

thumb   index   middle   ring

Chord Spelling

1st (D), ♭3rd (F), 5th (A)

Dm
Minor

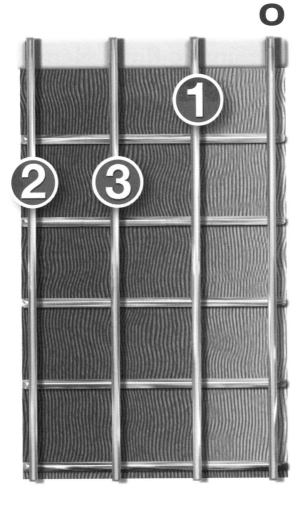

O

① ② ③

A   D   F   A

D

FREE ACCESS on smartphones including iPhone & Android

Using any QR code app scan and **HEAR** the chord on guitar and piano

D+
Augmented Triad

Simple Right Hand

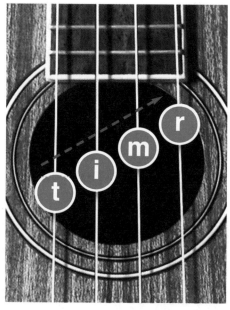

thumb   index   middle   ring

Chord Spelling

1st (D), 3rd (F♯), ♯5th (A♯)

A
A♯/B♭
B
C
C♯/D♭
D
D♯/E♭
E
F
F♯/G♭
G
G♯/A♭

D+
Augmented Triad

D

A♯   D   F♯   A♯

D°
Diminished Triad

Simple Right Hand

thumb   index   middle   ring

Chord Spelling

1st (D), ♭3rd (F), ♭5th (A♭)

A
A♯/B♭
B
C
C♯/D♭
D
D♯/E♭
E
F
F♯/G♭
G
G♯/A♭

D°
Diminished Triad

A♭   D   F   D

D

FREE ACCESS on smartphones including iPhone & Android   Using any QR code app scan and **HEAR** the chord on guitar and piano

Dsus2
Suspended 2nd

Simple Right Hand

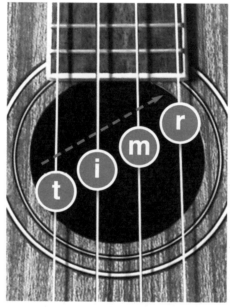

thumb   index   middle   ring

Chord Spelling
1st (D), 2nd (E), 5th (A)

FREE ACCESS on smartphones including iPhone & Android

Using any QR code app scan and **HEAR** the chord on guitar and piano

124

Dsus2
Suspended 2nd

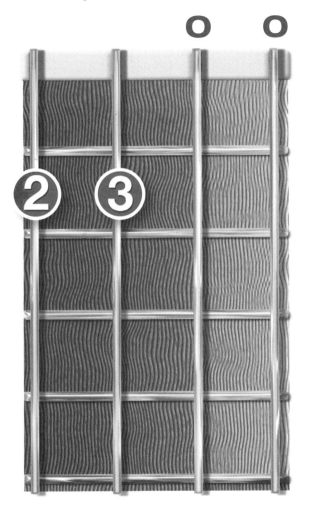

A D E A

D

Dsus4
Suspended 4th

Simple Right Hand

thumb   index   middle   ring

Chord Spelling

1st (D), 4th (G), 5th (A)

A
A#/Bb
B
C
C#/Db
D
D#/Eb
E
F
F#/Gb
G
G#/Ab

Dsus4
Suspended 4th

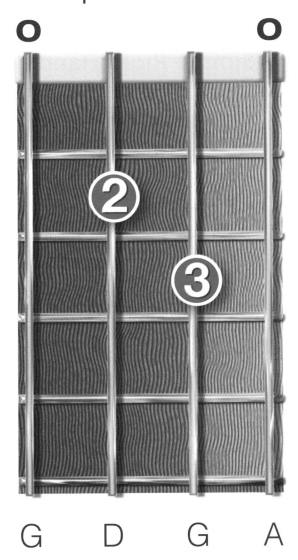

O   O

G   D   G   A

Using any QR code app scan and **HEAR** the chord on guitar and piano

D

D6
Major 6th

Simple Right Hand

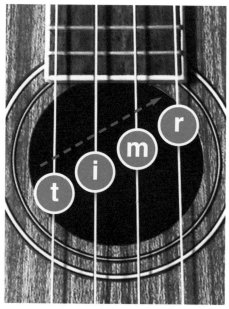

thumb   index   middle   ring

Chord Spelling

1st (D), 3rd (F#), 5th (A), 6th (B)

Using any QR code app scan and **HEAR** the chord on guitar and piano

A
A#/Bb
B
C
C#/Db
D
D#/Eb
E
F
F#/Gb
G
G#/Ab

D6
Major 6th

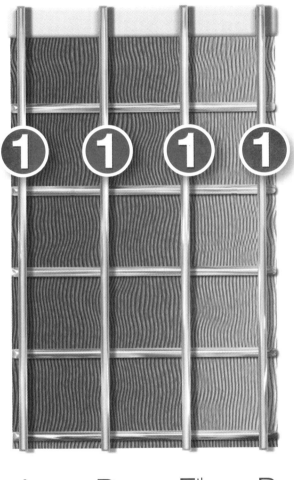

A   D   F♯   B

FREE ACCESS on smartphones including iPhone & Android

Using any QR code app scan and **HEAR** the chord on guitar and piano

Dmaj7
Major 7th

Simple Right Hand

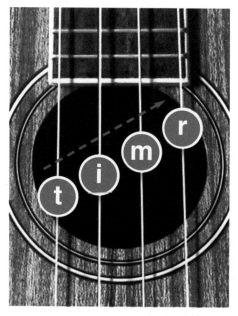

thumb   index   middle   ring

Chord Spelling

1st (D), 3rd (F♯), 5th (A), 7th (C♯)

FREE ACCESS on smartphones including iPhone & Android

Using any QR code app scan and **HEAR** the chord on guitar and piano

Dmaj7
Major 7th

A   D   F#   C#

D

FREE ACCESS on smartphones including iPhone & Android

Using any QR code app scan and **HEAR** the chord on guitar and piano

Dm7
Minor 7th

Simple Right Hand

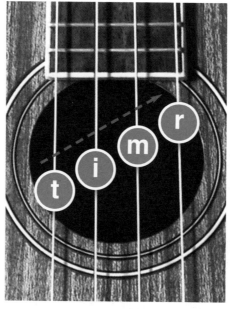

thumb   index   middle   ring

Chord Spelling

1st (D), ♭3rd (F), 5th (A), ♭7th (C)

Dm7
Minor 7th

Left Hand ✋

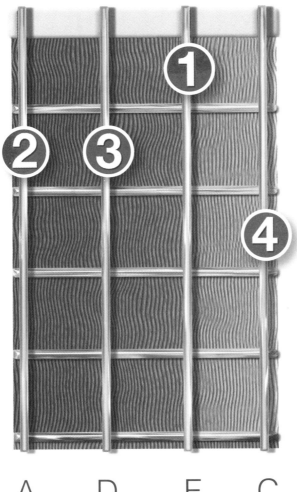

A   D   F   C

D

FREE ACCESS on smartphones including iPhone & Android

Using any QR code app scan and **HEAR** the chord on guitar and piano

D7
Dominant 7th

Simple Right Hand

thumb   index   middle   ring

Chord Spelling

1st (D), 3rd (F♯), 5th (A), ♭7th (C)

FREE ACCESS on smartphones
including iPhone & Android

Using any QR code app scan and **HEAR**
the chord on guitar and piano

A
A♯/B♭
B
C
C♯/D♭
D
D♯/E♭
E
F
F♯/G♭
G
G♯/A♭

D7
Dominant 7th

D

A   D   F♯   C

FREE ACCESS on smartphones including iPhone & Android

Using any QR code app scan and **HEAR** the chord on guitar and piano

D♯/E♭
Major

A

A♯/B♭

B

C

C♯/D♭

D

D♯/E♭

E

F

F♯/G♭

G

G♯/A♭

Simple Right Hand

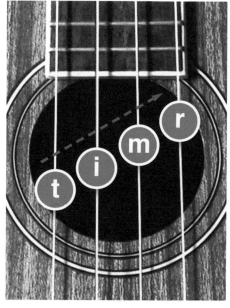

thumb   index   middle   ring

Chord Spelling

1st (E♭), 3rd (G), 5th (B♭)

D♯/E♭
Major

O

① ③ ④

G   E♭   G   B♭

D♯/E♭

D♯/E♭m
Minor

Simple Right Hand

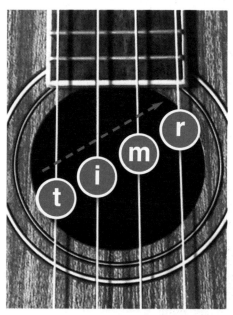

thumb   index   middle   ring

Chord Spelling

1st (E♭), ♭3rd (G♭), 5th (B♭)

A
A♯/B♭
B
C
C♯/D♭
D
D♯/E♭
E
F
F♯/G♭
G
G♯/A♭

D♯/E♭m
Minor

B♭   E♭   G♭   B♭

D♯/E♭

D♯/E♭+
Augmented Triad

Simple Right Hand

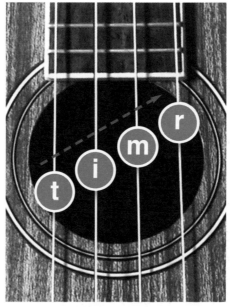

thumb   index   middle   ring

Chord Spelling

1st (E♭), 3rd (G), ♯5th (B)

FREE ACCESS on smartphones
including iPhone & Android

Using any QR code app scan and **HEAR**
the chord on guitar and piano

D♯/E♭+
Augmented Triad

G E♭ G B

D♯/E♭

141

D♯/E♭°
Diminished Triad

Simple Right Hand

thumb   index   middle   ring

Chord Spelling

1st (E♭), ♭3rd (G♭), ♭5th (B♭♭)

FREE ACCESS on smartphones including iPhone & Android

Using any QR code app scan and **HEAR** the chord on guitar and piano

A
A♯/B♭
B
C
C♯/D♭
D
D♯/E♭
E
F
F♯/G♭
G
G♯/A♭

D♯/E♭°
Diminished Triad

O

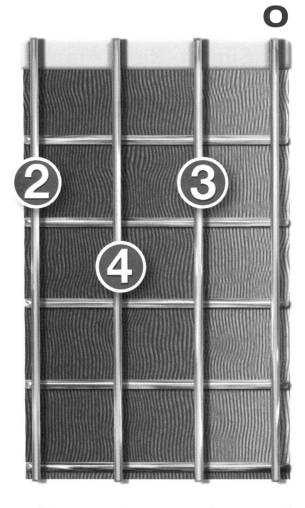

B𝄫   E♭   G♭   B𝄫

D♯/E♭

FREE ACCESS on smartphones including iPhone & Android

Using any QR code app scan and **HEAR** the chord on guitar and piano

D♯/E♭sus2
Suspended 2nd

Simple Right Hand

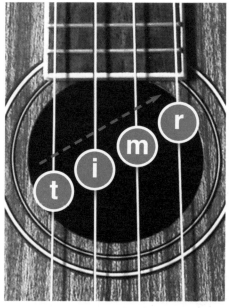

thumb   index   middle   ring

Chord Spelling

1st (E♭), 2nd (F), 5th (B♭)

D♯/E♭

D#/E♭sus2
Suspended 2nd

G   E♭   F   B♭

A
A♯/B♭
B
C
C♯/D♭
D
D♯/E♭
E
F
F♯/G♭
G
G♯/A♭

Right Hand

D♯/E♭sus4
Suspended 4th

Simple Right Hand

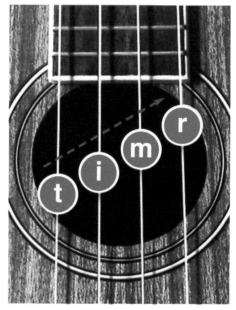

thumb   index   middle   ring

Chord Spelling

1st (E♭), 4th (A♭), 5th (B♭)

D♯/E♭

D♯/E♭sus4
Suspended 4th

D♯/E♭

Bb   Eb   Ab   Bb

D#/Eb6
Major 6th

Simple Right Hand

thumb　index　middle　ring

Chord Spelling

1st (Eb), 3rd (G), 5th (Bb), 6th (C)

Sidebar: A, A#/Bb, B, C, C#/Db, D, D#/Eb, E, F, F#/Gb, G, G#/Ab

D♯/E♭6
Major 6th

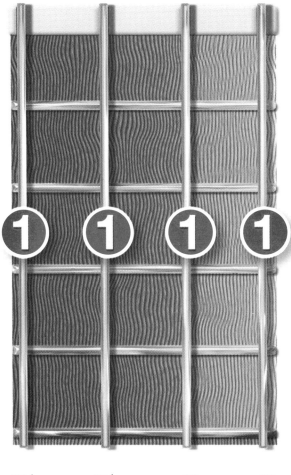

D♯/E♭

B♭   E♭   G   C

 Right Hand

D♯/E♭maj7
Major 7th

Simple Right Hand

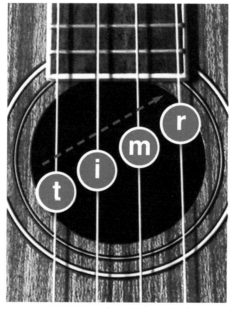

thumb   index   middle   ring

Chord Spelling

1st (E♭), 3rd (G), 5th (B♭), 7th (D)

D♯/E♭maj7
Major 7th

B♭ E♭ G D

D♯/E♭

D♯/E♭m7
Minor 7th

Simple Right Hand

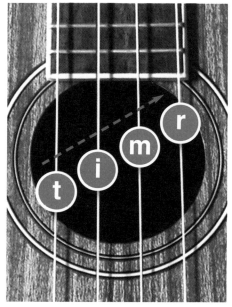

thumb   index   middle   ring

Chord Spelling

1st (E♭), ♭3rd (G♭), 5th (B♭), ♭7th (D♭)

D♯/E♭

D♯/E♭m7
Minor 7th

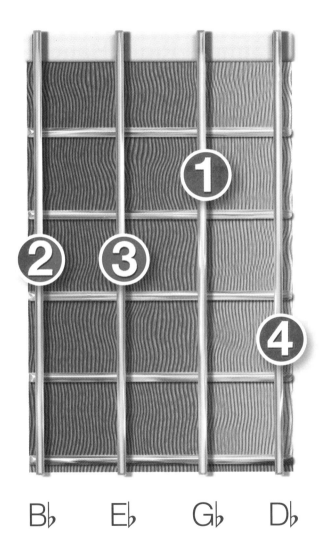

B♭   E♭   G♭   D♭

D♯/E♭

D#/E♭7
Dominant 7th

Simple Right Hand

thumb   index   middle   ring

Chord Spelling

1st (E♭), 3rd (G), 5th (B♭), ♭7th (D♭)

A
A#/B♭
B
C
C#/D♭
D
D#/E♭
E
F
F#/G♭
G
G#/A♭

D♯/E♭7
Dominant 7th

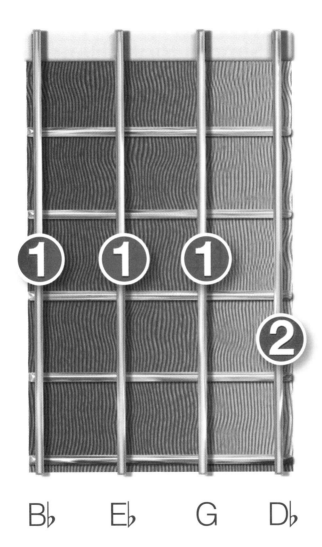

D♯/E♭

B♭   E♭   G   D♭

E
Major

Simple Right Hand

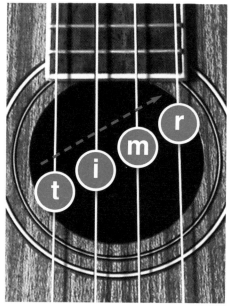

thumb   index   middle   ring

Chord Spelling

1st (E), 3rd (G♯), 5th (B)

E

E
Major

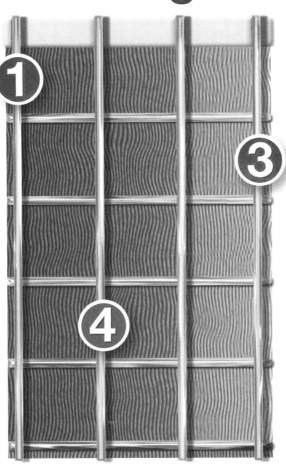

G♯   E   E   B

Using any QR code app scan and **HEAR** the chord on guitar and piano

E

Em
Minor

Simple Right Hand

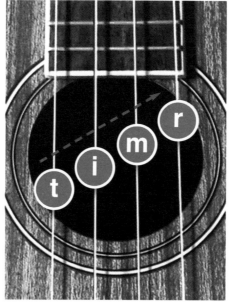

thumb   index   middle   ring

Chord Spelling

1st (E), ♭3rd (G), 5th (B)

Em
Minor

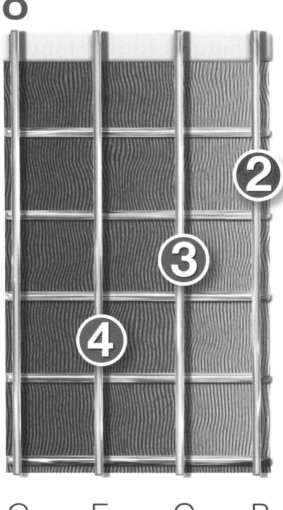

O

G   E   G   B

E

E+
Augmented Triad

Simple Right Hand

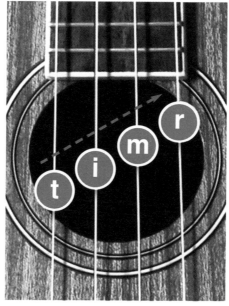

thumb   index   middle   ring

Chord Spelling

1st (E), 3rd (G#), #5th (B#)

E+
Augmented Triad

G♯   E   G♯   B♯

E

E°
Diminished Triad

Simple Right Hand

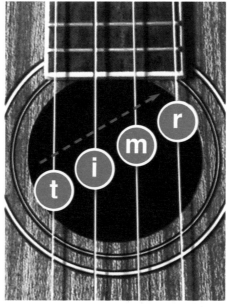

thumb index middle ring

Chord Spelling

1st (E), ♭3rd (G), ♭5th (B♭)

E°
Diminished Triad

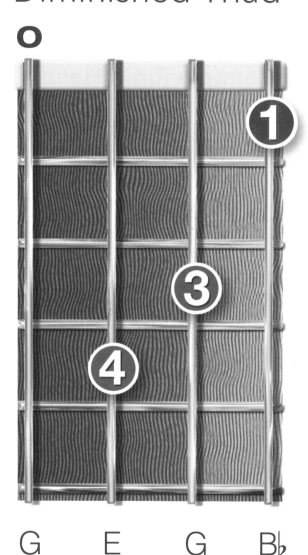

E

G   E   G   B♭

Esus2
Suspended 2nd

Simple Right Hand

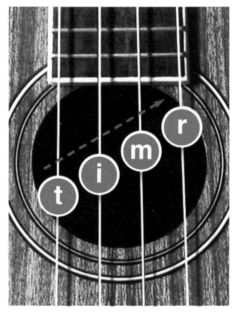

thumb   index   middle   ring

Chord Spelling

1st (E), 2nd (F♯), 5th (B)

Esus2
Suspended 2nd

B   E   F♯   B

E

Esus4
Suspended 4th

Simple Right Hand

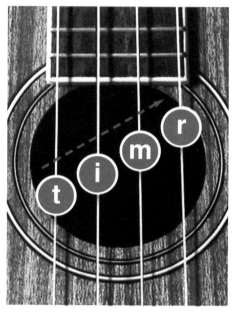

thumb   index   middle   ring

Chord Spelling
1st (E), 4th (A), 5th (B)

Esus4
Suspended 4th

O   O

③ ④

B   E   E   A

E

167

E6
Major 6th

Simple Right Hand

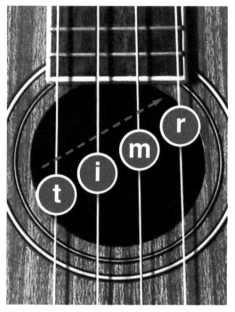

thumb   index   middle   ring

Chord Spelling

1st (E), 3rd (G#), 5th (B), 6th (C#)

FREE ACCESS on smartphones including iPhone & Android   Using any QR code app scan and **HEAR** the chord on guitar and piano

168

A
A#/Bb
B
C
C#/Db
D
D#/Eb
E
F
F#/Gb
G
G#/Ab

E6

Major 6th

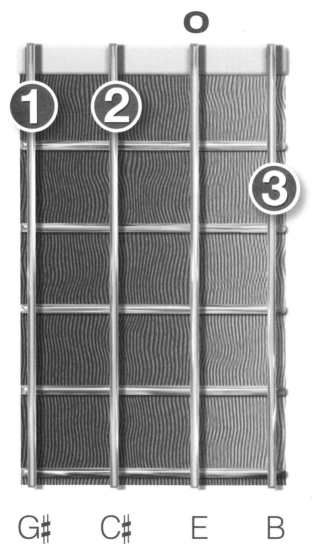

G#   C#   E   B

E

Emaj7
Major 7th

A
A#/B♭
B
C
C#/D♭
D
D#/E♭
E
F
F#/G♭
G
G#/A♭

Simple Right Hand

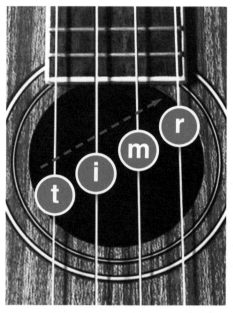

thumb   index   middle   ring

Chord Spelling
1st (E), 3rd (G#), 5th (B), 7th (D#)

Emaj7
Major 7th

Left Hand

G♯ D♯ E B

E

FREE ACCESS on smartphones
including iPhone & Android

Using any QR code app scan and **HEAR**
the chord on guitar and piano

Em7
Minor 7th

Simple Right Hand

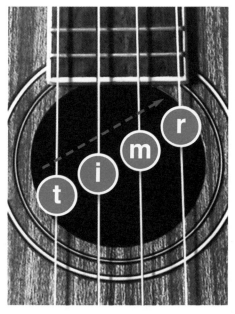

thumb　index　middle　ring

Chord Spelling
1st (E), ♭3rd (G), 5th (B), ♭7th (D)

Em7
Minor 7th

G   D   E   B

E

E7
Dominant 7th

Simple Right Hand

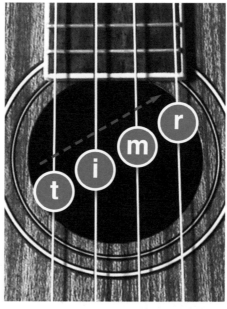

thumb   index   middle   ring

Chord Spelling
1st (E), 3rd (G♯), 5th (B), ♭7th (D)

E7
Dominant 7th

G♯   D   E   B

FREE ACCESS on smartphones including iPhone & Android

Using any QR code app scan and **HEAR** the chord on guitar and piano

F
Major

A
A♯/B♭
B
C
C♯/D♭
D
D♯/E♭
E
F
F♯/G♭
G
G♯/A♭

Simple Right Hand

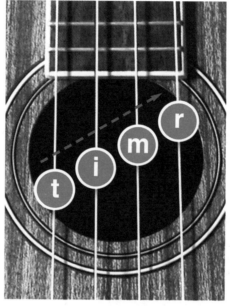

thumb   index   middle   ring

Chord Spelling
1st (F), 3rd (A), 5th (C)

FREE ACCESS on smartphones including iPhone & Android

Using any QR code app scan and **HEAR** the chord on guitar and piano

F
Major

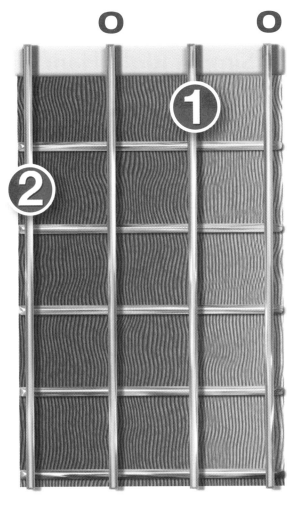

O   O

② ①

A   C   F   A

F

Fm
Minor

A

A♯/B♭

B

C

C♯/D♭

D

D♯/E♭

E

F

F♯/G♭

G

G♯/A♭

Simple Right Hand

thumb   index   middle   ring

Chord Spelling

1st (F), ♭3rd (A♭), 5th (C)

Fm
Minor

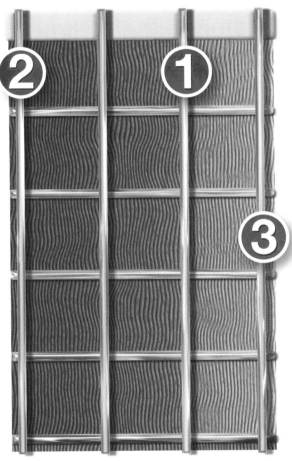

O

② ①

③

Ab C F C

F

Left Hand 🖐

F+
Augmented Triad

Simple Right Hand

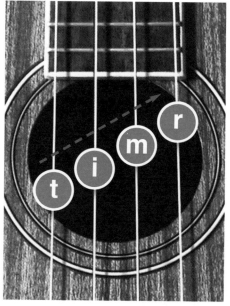

thumb   index   middle   ring

Chord Spelling

1st (F), 3rd (A), #5th (C#)

F+
Augmented Triad

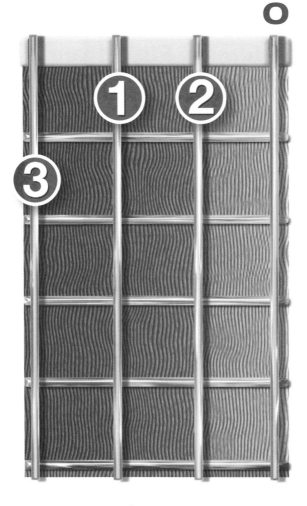

A   C♯   F   A

F°
Diminished Triad

Simple Right Hand

thumb　index　middle　ring

Chord Spelling
1st (F), ♭3rd (A♭), ♭5th (C♭)

A
A#/B♭
B
C
C#/D♭
D
D#/E♭
E
F
F#/G♭
G
G#/A♭

F°
Diminished Triad

C♭   F   A♭   C♭

F

Fsus2
Suspended 2nd

Simple Right Hand

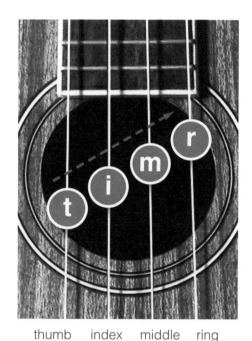

thumb   index   middle   ring

Chord Spelling
1st (F), 2nd (G), 5th (C)

Fsus2
Suspended 2nd

G   C   F   C

F

185

Fsus4
Suspended 4th

A
A#/Bb
B
C
C#/Db
D
D#/Eb
E
F
F#/Gb
G
G#/Ab

Simple Right Hand

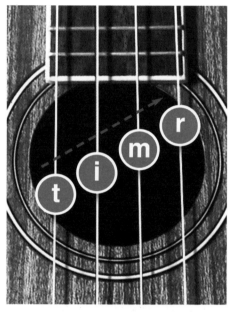

thumb   index   middle   ring

Chord Spelling

1st (F), 4th (Bb), 5th (C)

Fsus4
Suspended 4th

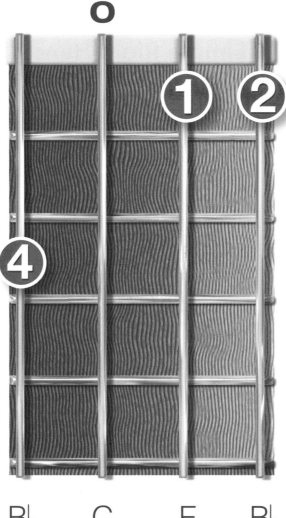

O

B♭   C   F   B♭

F

FREE ACCESS on smartphones
including iPhone & Android

Using any QR code app scan and **HEAR**
the chord on guitar and piano

 Right Hand

F6
Major 6th

Simple Right Hand

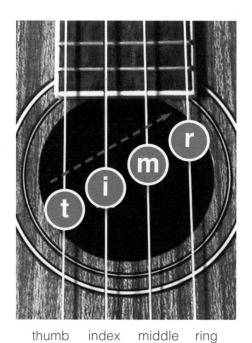

thumb   index   middle   ring

Chord Spelling
1st (F), 3rd (A), 5th (C), 6th (D)

A
A♯/B♭
B
C
C♯/D♭
D
D♯/E♭
E
F
F♯/G♭
G
G♯/A♭

F6
Major 6th

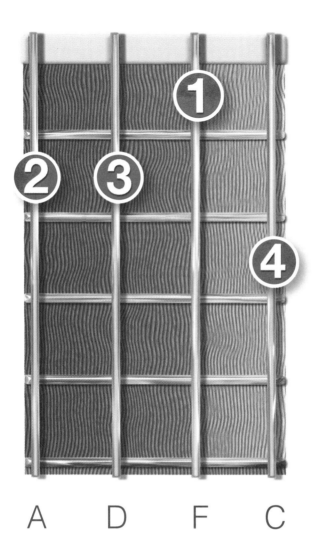

A   D   F   C

F

Fmaj7
Major 7th

Simple Right Hand

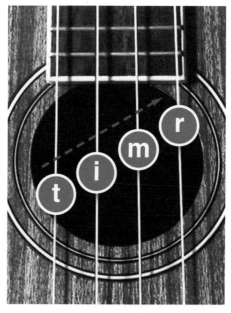

thumb   index   middle   ring

Chord Spelling

1st (F), 3rd (A), 5th (C), 7th (E)

A
A#/B♭
B
C
C#/D♭
D
D#/E♭
E
F
F#/G♭
G
G#/A♭

Fmaj7
Major 7th

A E F C

F

191

 Right Hand

Fm7
Minor 7th

Simple Right Hand

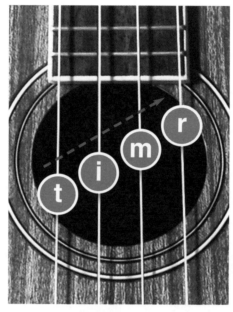

thumb   index   middle   ring

Chord Spelling

1st (F), ♭3rd (A♭), 5th (C), ♭7th (E♭)

A

A♯/B♭

B

C

C♯/D♭

D

D♯/E♭

E

F

F♯/G♭

G

G♯/A♭

FREE ACCESS on smartphones
including iPhone & Android

Using any QR code app scan and **HEAR**
the chord on guitar and piano

192

Fm7
Minor 7th

A♭   E♭   F   C

F

F7
Dominant 7th

Simple Right Hand

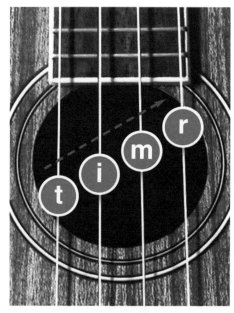

thumb   index   middle   ring

Chord Spelling

1st (F), 3rd (A), 5th (C), ♭7th (E♭)

A
A#/B♭
B
C
C#/D♭
D
D#/E♭
E
F
F#/G♭
G
G#/A♭

F7
Dominant 7th

A   E♭   F   C

F

F♯/G♭
Major

Simple Right Hand

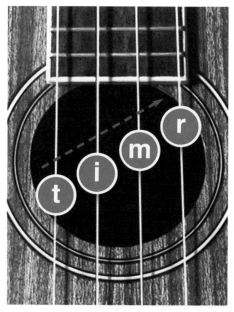

thumb   index   middle   ring

Chord Spelling

1st (F♯), 3rd (A♯), 5th (C♯)

F♯/G♭
Major

A♯   C♯   F♯   A♯

F♯/G♭

FREE ACCESS on smartphones
including iPhone & Android

Using any QR code app scan and **HEAR**
the chord on guitar and piano

F♯/G♭m
Minor

Simple Right Hand

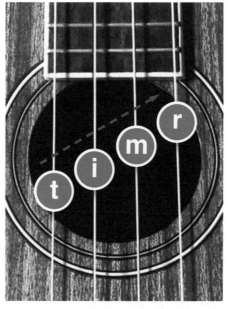

thumb index middle ring

Chord Spelling

1st (F♯), ♭3rd (A), 5th (C♯)

Using any QR code app scan and **HEAR** the chord on guitar and piano

A
A♯/B♭
B
C
C♯/D♭
D
D♯/E♭
E
F
F♯/G♭
G
G♯/A♭

F#/G♭m
Minor

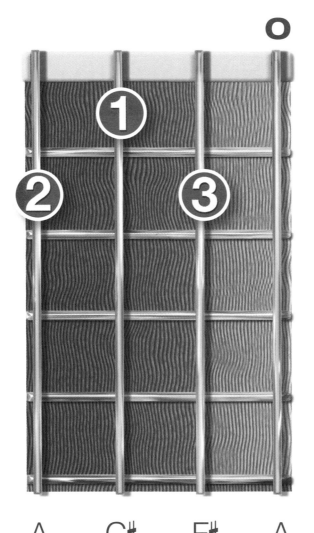

O

① ② ③

A   C#   F#   A

F#/G♭

F♯/G♭+
Augmented Triad

Simple Right Hand

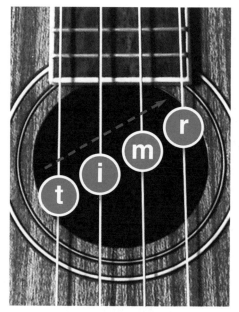

thumb   index   middle   ring

Chord Spelling
1st (F♯), 3rd (A♯), ♯5th (Cx)

F#/Gb+
Augmented Triad

A#   Cx   F#   A#

F#/Gb

F♯/G♭°
Diminished Triad

Simple Right Hand

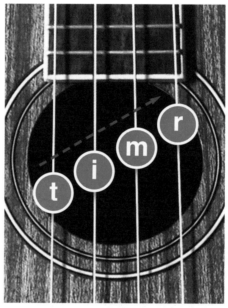

thumb index middle ring

Chord Spelling
1st (F♯), ♭3rd (A), ♭5th (C)

FREE ACCESS on smartphones including iPhone & Android — Using any QR code app scan and **HEAR** the chord on guitar and piano

F#/Gb°
Diminished Triad

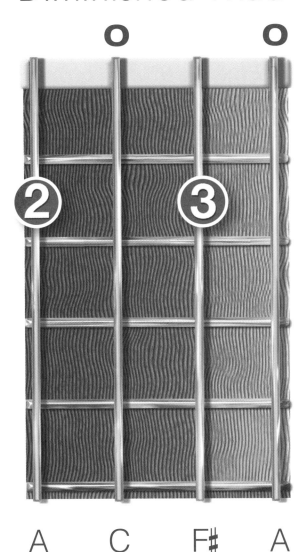

A   C   F#   A

F#/Gb

F#/G♭sus2
Suspended 2nd

Simple Right Hand

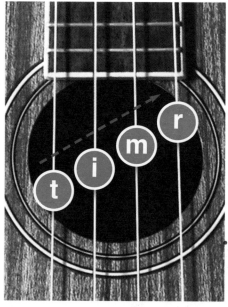

thumb   index   middle   ring

Chord Spelling

1st (F#), 2nd (G#), 5th (C#)

A

A#/B♭

B

C

C#/D♭

D

D#/E♭

E

F

F#/G♭

G

G#/A♭

F#/G♭sus2
Suspended 2nd

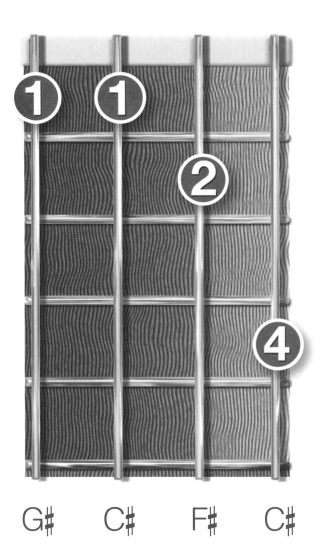

G#   C#   F#   C#

F#/G♭

F#/G♭sus4
Suspended 4th

Simple Right Hand

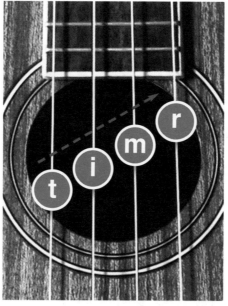

thumb   index   middle   ring

Chord Spelling

1st (F#), 4th (B), 5th (C#)

Sidebar: A A#/B♭ B C C#/D♭ D D#/E♭ E F F#/G♭ G G#/A♭

F#/G♭sus4
Suspended 4th

B   C#   F#   B

F#/G♭

Right Hand

F♯/G♭6
Major 6th

Simple Right Hand

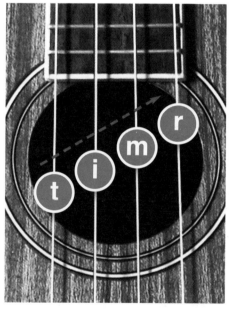

thumb index middle ring

Chord Spelling

1st (F♯), 3rd (A♯), 5th (C♯), 6th (D♯)

A
A♯/B♭
B
C
C♯/D♭
D
D♯/E♭
E
F
F♯/G♭
G
G♯/A♭

FREE ACCESS on smartphones including iPhone & Android

Using any QR code app scan and **HEAR** the chord on guitar and piano

208

F#/Gb6
Major 6th

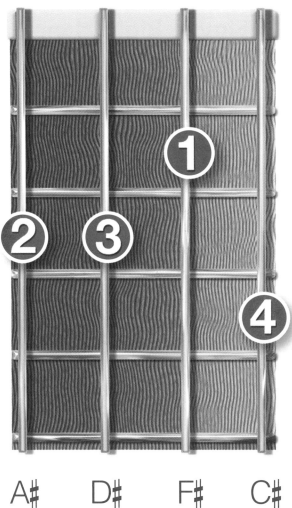

A#   D#   F#   C#

F#/Gb

Right Hand

F#/G♭maj7
Major 7th

Simple Right Hand

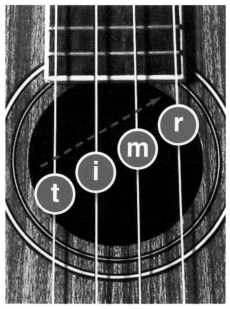

thumb   index   middle   ring

Chord Spelling

1st (F#), 3rd (A#), 5th (C#), 7th (E#)

F#/G♭maj7
Major 7th

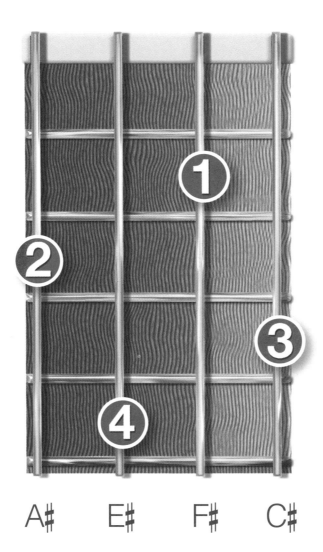

A#   E#   F#   C#

F#/G♭

F#/G♭m7
Minor 7th

Simple Right Hand

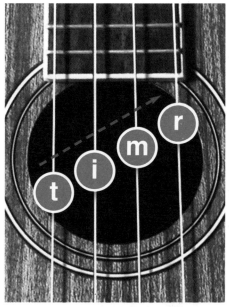

thumb   index   middle   ring

Chord Spelling

1st (F#), ♭3rd (A), 5th (C#), ♭7th (E)

A

A#/B♭

B

C

C#/D♭

D

D#/E♭

E

F

F#/G♭

G

G#/A♭

F#/G♭m7
Minor 7th

A   E   F#   C#

F#/G♭

F♯/G♭7
Dominant 7th

Simple Right Hand

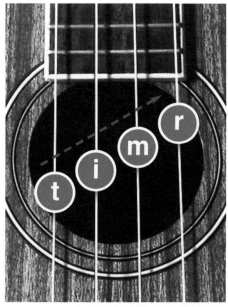

thumb   index   middle   ring

Chord Spelling

1st (F♯), 3rd (A♯), 5th (C♯), ♭7th (E)

A
A♯/B♭
B
C
C♯/D♭
D
D♯/E♭
E
F
F♯/G♭
G
G♯/A♭

F♯/G♭7
Dominant 7th

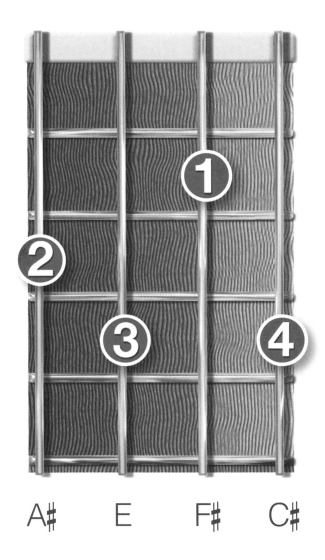

A♯   E   F♯   C♯

F♯/G♭

G
Major

A
A#/B♭
B
C
C#/D♭
D
D#/E♭
E
F
F#/G♭
G
G#/A♭

Simple Right Hand

thumb　index　middle　ring

Chord Spelling
1st (G), 3rd (B), 5th (D)

G
Major

O

G D G B

Left Hand 🖐

G

Gm
Minor

Simple Right Hand

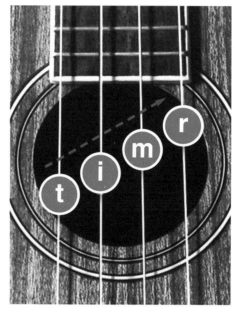

thumb index middle ring

Chord Spelling

1st (G), ♭3rd (B♭), 5th (D)

G

Gm
Minor

O

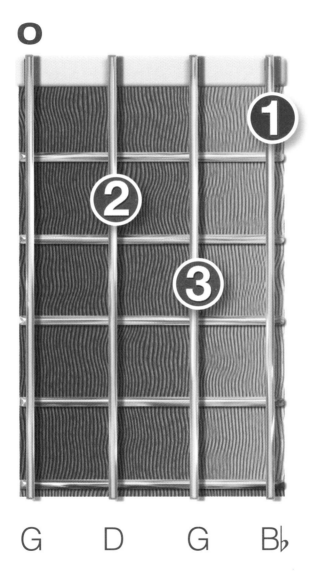

G   D   G   B♭

G

G+
Augmented Triad

Simple Right Hand

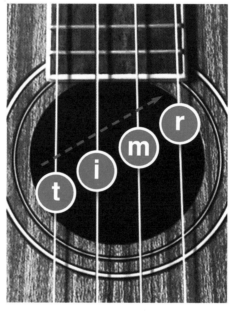

thumb   index   middle   ring

Chord Spelling

1st (G), 3rd (B), #5th (D#)

FREE ACCESS on smartphones including iPhone & Android

Using any QR code app scan and **HEAR** the chord on guitar and piano

G+
Augmented Triad

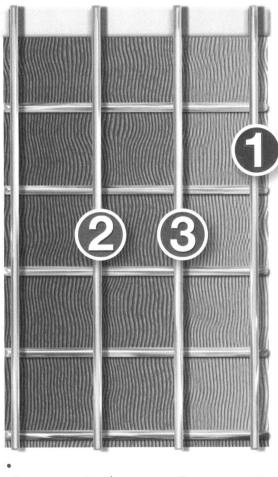

G   D♯   G   B

G

G°
Diminished Triad

Simple Right Hand

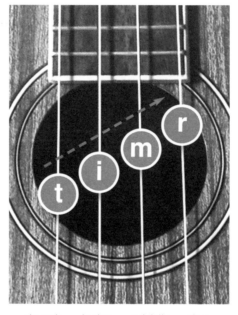

thumb   index   middle   ring

Chord Spelling

1st (G), ♭3rd (B♭), ♭5th (D♭)

G°
Diminished Triad

O

① ② ③

G   Db   G   Bb

G

FREE ACCESS on smartphones
including iPhone & Android

Using any QR code app scan and **HEAR**
the chord on guitar and piano

223

 Right Hand

Gsus2
Suspended 2nd

Simple Right Hand

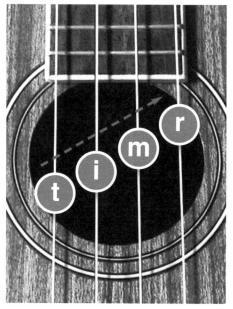

thumb   index   middle   ring

Chord Spelling

1st (G), 2nd (A), 5th (D)

G

 Using any QR code app scan and **HEAR**
the chord on guitar and piano

Gsus2

Suspended 2nd

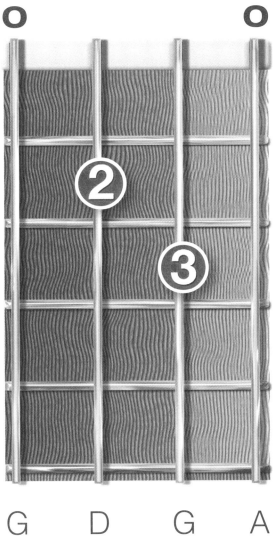

G   D   G   A

G

FREE ACCESS on smartphones
including iPhone & Android

Using any QR code app scan and **HEAR**
the chord on guitar and piano

Gsus4
Suspended 4th

Simple Right Hand

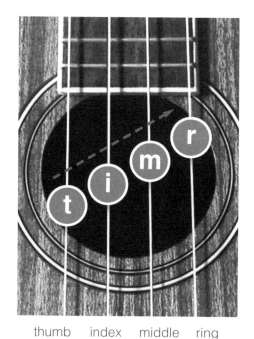

thumb   index   middle   ring

Chord Spelling

1st (G), 4th (C), 5th (D)

Gsus4
Suspended 4th

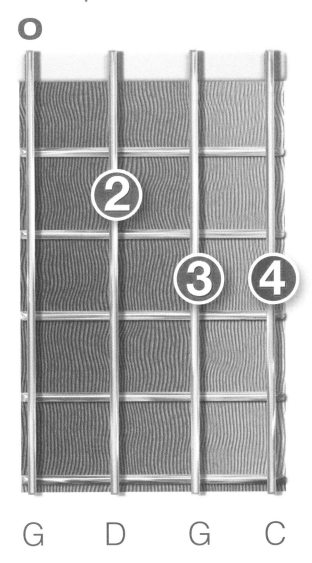

G   D   G   C

G

G6
Major 6th

Simple Right Hand

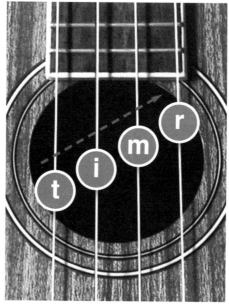

thumb   index   middle   ring

Chord Spelling

1st (G), 3rd (B), 5th (D), 6th (E)

FREE ACCESS on smartphones
including iPhone & Android

Using any QR code app scan and **HEAR**
the chord on guitar and piano

G6
Major 6th

O · · O · ·

G D E B

G

Gmaj7
Major 7th

Simple Right Hand

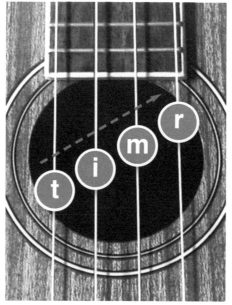

thumb   index   middle   ring

Chord Spelling

1st (G), 3rd (B), 5th (D), 7th (F♯)

 G

Gmaj7
Major 7th

G   D   F♯   B

G

FREE ACCESS on smartphones
including iPhone & Android

Using any QR code app scan and **HEAR**
the chord on guitar and piano

Gm7
Minor 7th

Simple Right Hand

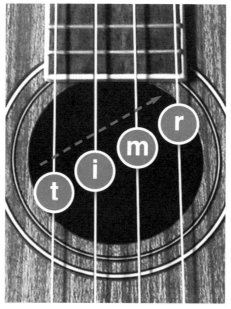

thumb   index   middle   ring

Chord Spelling

1st (G), ♭3rd (B♭), 5th (D), ♭7th (F)

G

Gm7
Minor 7th

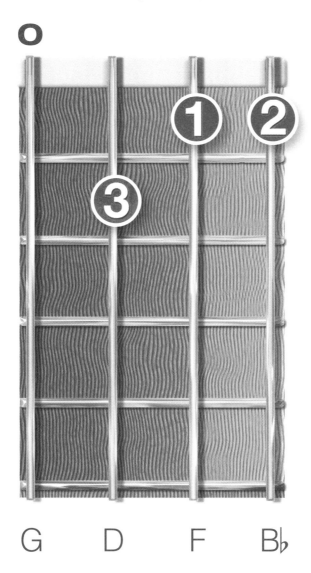

G   D   F   B♭

G

G7
Dominant 7th

Simple Right Hand

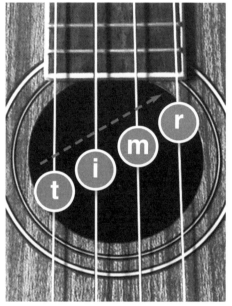

thumb   index   middle   ring

Chord Spelling

1st (G), 3rd (B), 5th (D), ♭7th (F)

G

G7
Dominant 7th

O

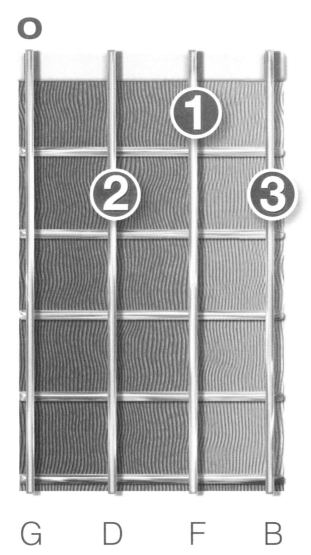

G   D   F   B

G

235

G♯/A♭
Major

Simple Right Hand

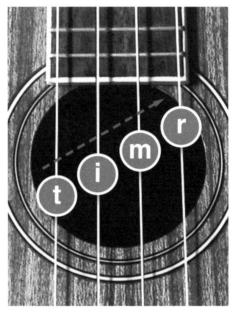

thumb   index   middle   ring

Chord Spelling

1st (A♭), 3rd (C), 5th (E♭)

G♯/A♭

G♯/A♭
Major

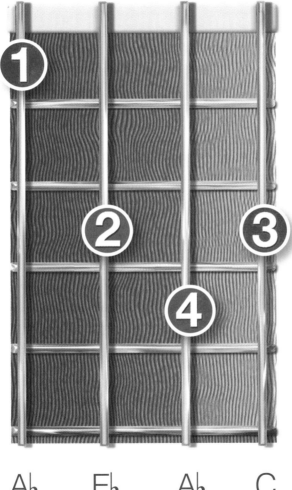

A♭   E♭   A♭   C

G♯/A♭

G#/A♭m
Minor

Simple Right Hand

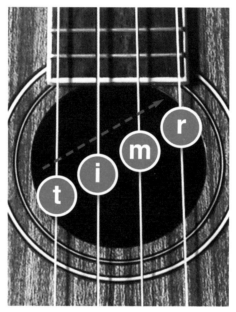

thumb   index   middle   ring

Chord Spelling

1st (A♭), ♭3rd (C♭), 5th (E♭)

G#/A♭

G♯/A♭m
Minor

A♭   E♭   A♭   C♭

239

G♯/A♭

G♯/A♭+
Augmented Triad

Simple Right Hand

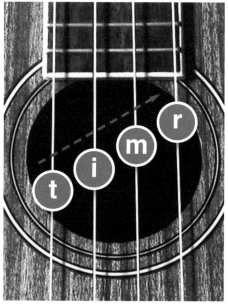

thumb   index   middle   ring

Chord Spelling

1st (A♭), 3rd (C), ♯5th (E)

G♯/A♭

G♯/A♭+
Augmented Triad

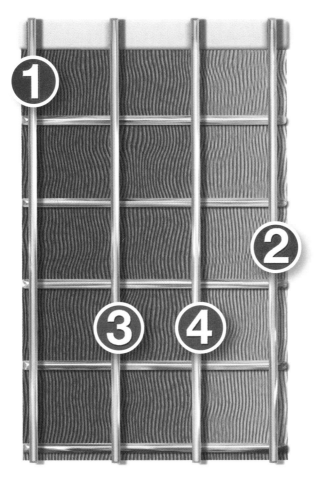

A♭   E   A♭   C

Using any QR code app scan and **HEAR** the chord on guitar and piano

G♯/A♭

241

G♯/A♭°
Diminished Triad

Simple Right Hand

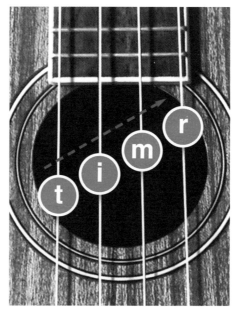

thumb   index   middle   ring

Chord Spelling

1st (A♭), ♭3rd (C♭), ♭5th (E♭♭)

G♯/A♭°
Diminished Triad

A♭   E♭♭   A♭   C♭

G♯/A♭

243

 Right Hand

G♯/A♭sus2
Suspended 2nd

Simple Right Hand

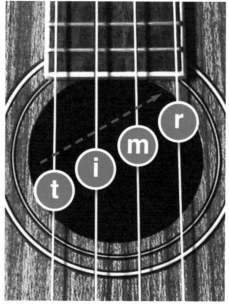

thumb   index   middle   ring

Chord Spelling

1st (A♭), 2nd (B♭), 5th (E♭)

G♯/A♭

FREE ACCESS on smartphones
including iPhone & Android

Using any QR code app scan and **HEAR**
the chord on guitar and piano

244

G♯/A♭sus2
Suspended 2nd

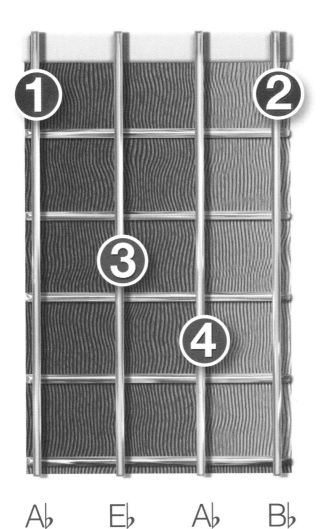

A♭   E♭   A♭   B♭

FREE ACCESS on smartphones
including iPhone & Android

Using any QR code app scan and **HEAR**
the chord on guitar and piano

G♯/A♭

G#/A♭sus4
Suspended 4th

Simple Right Hand

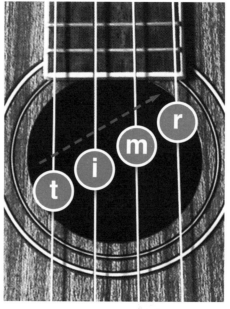

thumb   index   middle   ring

Chord Spelling

1st (A♭), 4th (D♭), 5th (E♭)

A
A#/B♭
B
C
C#/D♭
D
D#/E♭
E
F
F#/G♭
G
G#/A♭

G#/A♭sus4
Suspended 4th

A♭   E♭   A♭   D♭

G#/A♭

 Right Hand

G#/Ab6
Major 6th

Simple Right Hand

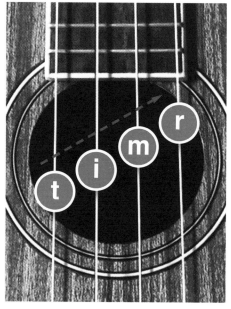

thumb   index   middle   ring

Chord Spelling

1st (Ab), 3rd (C), 5th (Eb), 6th (F)

G#/Ab

G#/A♭6
Major 6th

A♭   E♭   F   C

G#/A♭

G♯/A♭maj7
Major 7th

Simple Right Hand

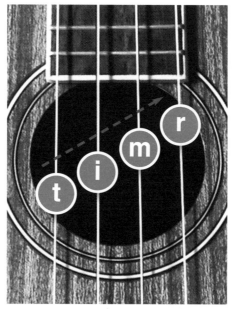

thumb   index   middle   ring

Chord Spelling

1st (A♭), 3rd (C), 5th (E♭), 7th (G)

G♯/A♭

G♯/A♭maj7
Major 7th

A♭   E♭   G   C

FREE ACCESS on smartphones including iPhone & Android

Using any QR code app scan and **HEAR** the chord on guitar and piano

G♯/A♭

251

G♯/A♭m7
Minor 7th

Simple Right Hand

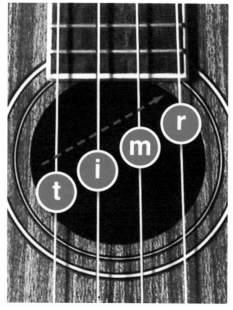

thumb   index   middle   ring

Chord Spelling

1st (A♭), ♭3rd (C♭), 5th (E♭), ♭7th (G♭)

G♯/A♭m7

Minor 7th

A♭   E♭   G♭   C♭

G♯/A♭

G#/A♭7
Dominant 7th

Simple Right Hand

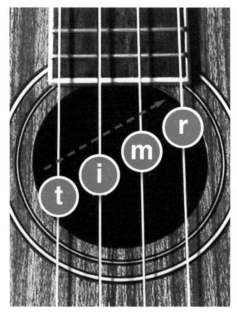

thumb   index   middle   ring

Chord Spelling

1st (A♭), 3rd (C), 5th (E♭), ♭7th (G♭)

G♯/A♭7
Dominant 7th

| ① | ② | ③ | ④ |

A♭   E♭   G♭   C

G♯/A♭

UKULELE CHORDS MADE EASY

A new title in our best-selling series, designed for players of all abilities and ages. Created for musicians by musicians, these books offer a quick and practical resource for those playing on their own or with a band. They work equally well for the rock and indie musician as they do for the jazz, folk, country, blues or classical enthusiast.

The MUSIC MADE EASY series

See it and Hear it! Comprehensive sound links

Guitar Chords Made Easy, Left Hand Guitar Chords Made Easy, Piano and Keyboard Chords Made Easy, Scales and Modes Made Easy, Reading Music Made Easy, Learn to Play Piano Made Easy, Learn to Play Guitar Made Easy.

The SPIRAL, EASY-TO-USE series

Advanced Guitar Chords; Advanced Piano Chords; Guitar Chords; Piano & Keyboard Chords; Chords for Kids; Play Flamenco; How to Play Guitar; How to Play Bass Guitar; How to Play Classic Riffs; Songwriter's Rhyming Dictionary; How to Become a Star; How to Read Music; How to Write Great Songs; How to Play Rhythm, Riffs & Lead Rock; How to Play Hard, Metal & Nu Rock; How to Make Music on the Web; My First Recorder Music; Piano Sheet Music; Brass & Wind Sheet Music; Scales & Modes; Beginners' Guide to Reading Music.

For further information on these titles please visit our trading website:
www.flametreepublishing.com

www.flametreemusic.com

Practical information on chords, scales, riffs, rhymes and instruments through a growing combination of traditional print books and ebooks. Features over **1800 chords**, with **sound files** for notes and strummed chords.